The Duesenberg

The Story of America's Premier Car

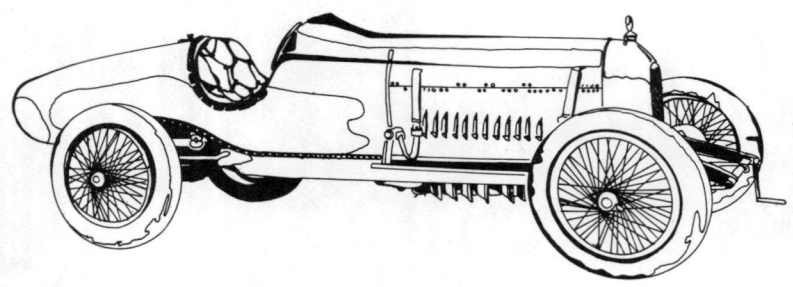

The Duesenberg

Louis William Steinwedel
J. Herbert Newport

Chilton Book Company
Philadelphia New York London

Copyright © 1970 by Louis William Steinwedel
and J. Herbert Newport
First Edition
All rights reserved
Published in Philadelphia by Chilton Book Company
and simultaneously in Ontario, Canada,
by Thomas Nelson & Sons, Ltd.
ISBN 0–8019–5559–9
Library of Congress Catalog Card Number 73–133030

Designed by Cypher Associates, Inc.
Manufactured in the United States of America
by The Plimpton Press

Contents

Chapter 1 The Dawn of the Duesenberg 1
Chapter 2 The Straight Eight Is Born 8
Chapter 3 The Model A 17
Chapter 4 The Mighty Model "J" 34
Chapter 5 The Duesenberg Look 71
Chapter 6 Duesenberg at Speed 121
Chapter 7 The Legend Lives On 145

Acknowledgments

We wish to thank the following people for their help in compiling the photographs and information which made this book a pleasure to write:

Harold T. Ames	Bill Kinsman
Syd Ayers	Joe Knapp
Scott Bailey	Charley Mooney
Gordon Buehrig	John North
Pete De Paolo	Bill Pettit
Jim Dougherty	Lou Reinke
Al Ferrara	Harry Resnick
Jerry Gebby	Rick Simpson
Dick Greene	Ron Stuckey
Bill Harrah	Pete Warvel
Dr. Erle Heath	Ray Wolff
Frank Hershey	Phil Wright
Jim Hoe	Gene Zimmerman
Royce Kershaw	

The Duesenberg

1

The Dawn of the Duesenberg

The Duesenberg automobile holds the unique distinction of being the most outstanding car ever built on the North American continent . . . America's premier car. Webster defines "premier" as "principal" or "of the first rank" which is an accurate description of Duesenberg's place on the road in its halycon days of the 1930s. Actually, the passage of the better part of half a century has not done much to challenge Duesenberg's place as the premier American automobile. Certainly no current production Detroit car can measure up to its self-assured image of elegance and excellence, to the clean lines, or to the fine finish and meticulous attention to detail that went into its building. And rather few contemporary American cars, despite a lot of intervening engineering, can match Duesenberg for sheer performance: 0 to 100 MPH in seventeen seconds, 104 MPH in second gear, and a top speed of 129 MPH with three tons on board.

To someone who had never heard of it before, a big, powerful car called "Duesenberg" is likely to conjure up images of exciting speed on the autobahn or of haughtily drawing up in front of a fashionable casino on the Riviera. Duesenberg was

THE DUESENBERG

an exotic, foreign sounding name not unlike those of the great European luxury marques, a coincidence which probably did not hurt sales one bit in the prestige-conscious circles where Duesenberg customarily did business. The mistaken European aura managed to persist even through the publicity-filled "golden era" of the thirties, at least enough to permit a side show proprietor to tour the middle west after World War II with a "J" type Duesenberg, charging the local citizenry to see "Hitler's car". Apparently, no one got to see the name plate marked "Indianapolis, Indiana".

The Duesenberg story couldn't have had a more American origin, beginning "where the tall corn grows" in the very heartland of America. Although Fred Duesenberg was born in Germany—a few months after General Custer fell at the Little Big Horn—he came to the American frontier as a small child. The seven Duesenberg children, four boys and three girls, lived a modest, typical Iowa farm life in the 1880s which could have been lifted intact out of a Willa Cather novel. Here, young Fred and August Duesenberg absorbed the virtues of Victorian America which would still be evident years later in their honest, sturdy, "built to last" machines.

However, farm life and growing things in the rich Iowa soil did not submerge the boys' interest in gadgets, and the Teutonic love of mechanics sprouted and blossomed early. It was Fred who emerged as the natural engineer of the two, with August at his side giving suggestions and encouragement and learning from his brother. Fred Duesenberg was ten years old when Gottlieb Daimler and Karl Benz ran the first successful internal combustion vehicles in Germany in 1886, an event probably unheralded in the bucolic little Iowa town, but one which held great potential for the Duesenberg brothers. As a teenager, Fred's fascination with "things that ran" was already carrying him away from farm life; although not too far, for his first job was as a mechanic repairing farm equipment.

The Dawn of the Duesenberg

It did not take Fred and August too long to turn their attention to wheeled vehicles. Soon they had a small business repairing, building, and racing bicycles, curiously a beginning they had in common with the Wright brothers. Fred learned early that racing his product brought interest and sales, and before he parted company with the two wheelers he had established two world's records with his bikes.

Appropriately, in the first year of the twentieth century Duesenberg decided that wheels should be turned by internal combustion engines rather than muscle power. It was a time when the infant automobile was just beginning to make an impression on the American scene. In 1894 a French newspaper called *Le Petit Journal* had organized the world's first automobile race from Paris to Rouen, and the following year the thrill of pioneer car racing came to America when the *Chicago Times-Herald* sponsored a similar eighty-five-mile race of spidery looking "motorcycles" through the snowy streets of Chicago on Thanksgiving Day. Part of the purpose of the contest ($500 worth) was to select a name for the new self-propelled vehicles. "Motor wagon" was unwieldy and sounded too much like the German *Motor-wagen. Automobile* was entirely too French for mid-Western tastes. So, "motorcycles" they were. It must have been some encouragement to the young Duesenbergs to see that another motor-minded pair of brothers, the Duryeas from Massachusetts, won America's first automobile race on what is generally credited as America's first car.

In the earliest days of the automobile the only way to build one was by guesswork, trial and error, and blind faith. Fred Duesenberg was lucky enough to come on the scene when there were at least places where he could go to learn how to build an automobile. One of those places was a struggling young company in Wisconsin which was building a small car called the Rambler, and it was here that Fred Duesenberg put

The Duesenberg

in his internship as a budding creator of cars. Then, his head crammed with techniques and ideas, he came back home to Iowa (this time to the "big city"—Des Moines) and opened a garage to compete with the only other one in town.

The little garage prospered modestly, but Fred Duesenberg's thoughts were already a full step ahead. He wanted to create a car of his own; not just a little Rambler-type runabout but a racer like the fast French and German cars that Willie K. Vanderbilt and his pals ran on the good roads of Long Island. A frequent visitor to Fred's shop in Des Moines was a lawyer named Mason whom the young mechanic managed to infect with the rampaging germs of "automania". Deserting Kent and Blackstone, Mason became a Duesenberg disciple and put up the money for "the First Duesenberg" of 1903, which translated as "The Mason Motor Car".

The car which emerged from the partnership was hardly what the Southampton set was running back East, but it was a relatively fast and tough, and typically American, little machine produced at small cost. The Mason was an opposed twin-cylinder car with a 5 x 5-inch bore and stroke and was rated at 24 horsepower. Its builder promised 40 MPH and the ability to "take any hill on high gear". With Fred at the wheel, the Mason quickly made a name for itself on the dirt tracks in the middle of America. In fact, the name was so good and the public interest so high that it became evident that Mason's name would grace something more lucrative than the winners' list at county fairs.

The Mason Motor Car Company was founded in Des Moines in 1904 and began to market a production version of Fred's two-cylinder car. Judging from contemporary advertising for the car—which was anything but reticent about its virtues—the Mason was a desirable piece of machinery for the $1250 base price. An early ad claimed it to be "The fastest and strongest two-cylinder car in America", and related that "At the first hill

The Dawn of the Duesenberg

climbing contest of the Iowa Automobile Association held at Des Moines on July 4th, 1906, the Mason won easily against all competitors including a four-cylinder car listing at $4000 and rated at forty horsepower." A later ad waxed bolder: "Take a ride in all the other cars, then ride in the Mason. We will guarantee it to do everything any other car does regardless of horsepower, and do it better."

Neither Mason, the entrepreneur, nor Duesenberg, the self-made engineer, were destined to become Henry Fords with their little car. After a half dozen years of business, Mason's company was acquired in 1910 by a businessman named Frederick L. Maytag (of washing machine fame) and the new firm was re-organized as The Maytag Mason Motor Company. Operations were moved to Waterloo, Iowa. The new management placed emphasis on production and sales, none on racing. Accordingly, they promptly lost the interest and services of one Frederick S. Duesenberg.

Actually, the departure from Mason came at an appropriate time, for Duesenberg had outgrown his debut effort into the automotive world. He had bigger and better things in mind. By 1910, two-cylinder automobile engines were archaic and obsolete. There was a lesson to be learned from one of the pioneers of the automobile, Karl Benz, who was for awhile satisfied to refine his original twin-cylinder concepts and as a result watched other more progressive builders whittle away his hold on the market. Duesenberg realized that the kind of speed he was interested in wasn't going to come from a two-cylinder engine. In fact, what he had in mind went well beyond the ordinary L-head and T-head four-cylinder powerplants that were the rule of the day in 1910.

After the Mason venture, Duesenberg turned his talents to designing an entirely new four-cylinder engine which was to have profound effect in establishing the Duesenberg name as a power to be reckoned with. Like Ettore Bugatti, Fred Duesenberg had little formal technical training but he had a natural talent for mechanics and an incisive ability to select the right shape or size of a part. For instance, there were times when he would rattle off the dimensions of a key engine part while glancing at a gauge in his hand. Later, precise computations showed that the part had to be within a few thousandths of an inch of Duesenberg's apparently off-handed guess! Again like Bugatti, Duesenberg's natural mechanical talents rather than schooled disciplines gave him the freedom to try what formal engineers knew to be "foolish" or "impossible".

Such was the case with his new engine with its rectangular combustion chambers and horizontal valves operated by unorthodox vertical rocker arms nearly a foot long! It was a peculiar looking piece of machinery to say the least and at first glance probably caused both novice and professional to shake their heads in disbelief and mystery. The new Duesenberg four-cylinder was, however, upon close analysis a rather more efficient engine than most of its contemporaries, owing to its compact combustion space and its ability to concentrate most of the power directly upon the piston head. In 1913, The Duesenberg Motor Company was set up in St. Paul, Minnesota, to build the engine for both automotive and marine use.

The *raison d'etre* of the new machine was well beyond transporting well-to-do Iowa farmers into town on Saturday night, as the Mason had done. Neither did Fred Duesenberg have in mind his old proving grounds, the Iowa dirt tracks, but rather the new brick paved circuit at Indianapolis. Five hundred miles over the Indy bricks was the ultimate American challenge for both car and driver, and immortality awaited both man and machine that could make it. Duesenberg believed he had both the machine, in his new "walking beam" four-cylinder, and the man, in a young fellow named Eddie Rickenbacker.

Champagne was a little premature, however, for Ricken-

The Dawn of the Duesenberg

backer's Duesenberg came in nine places behind the winning Delage, despite a performance which was a model of regularity and a prediction of things to come. Rickenbacker's "number 10" Duesenberg has been carefully restored under the direction of the Indianapolis Speedway Museum director Karl Kizer and is now one of the museum's proudest displays. Duesenbergs would run again at Indianapolis but their pre-World War I ill luck would hold. In 1915, a pair of Duesenberg captured fifth and tenth places, yielding first honors to Ralph DePalma's 1914 Grand Prix Mercedes. The next year Duesenberg moved up to second spot, topped only by the great Dario Resta driving the Ernest Henry-designed, twin-cam Peugeot Grand Prix car.

The year before the United States went to war, the Duesenberg brothers moved their plant to Elizabeth, New Jersey, and soon got their first U.S. Government contract to build the "walking beam" engine for use in light training planes. By this time, they had developed the original engine to a degree of sophistication which gave it four valves per cylinder operated by two camshafts. The move from Minnesota to New Jersey in a sense marked the passing of an era and the start of a new one for Duesenberg. The pioneer days were behind them now. The rough edges, both technical and administrative, had been polished and the brothers Duesenberg were ready to step into that new era and conquer it with undreamed of glamour.

2

The Straight Eight is Born

In 1917, the United States was at war, and embarrassingly without the implements to carry the fight into the clouds over France. As the French Grand Prix of 1914 had convincingly demonstrated, with the aero-inspired engines in the Mercedes Grand Prix cars spectacularly sweeping the field 1-2-3, European engine development had leaped far ahead of what was going on on this side of the Atlantic. With the war at hand, American industry suddenly appreciated the European advances and sought to learn from them, duplicate and improve them, and then mass produce the finished product as only American industry had learned how. A good, typical case in point was the famous "Liberty" aero engine, the most well known of the American World War I "flying machine" powerplants. It was an open secret that the "Liberty" was a watered down version of the 1914 Mercedes Grand Prix engine concept, substituting two valves per cylinder for the original four and using a modified type of the Mercedes welded-on water jacket. The inspiration had come directly from Ralph DePalma's Mercedes racer which had vanished into the Packard factory not long after it took the 1915 Indianapolis 500.

The Straight Eight Is Born

To develop its own engines of equivalent sophistication would cost the American war effort precious time which it could ill afford. So, to short-cut much original experimentation, the United States Government sent a commission to Paris to study what the French were doing in aero engines, to see what could be adapted to American use, and possibly to adopt some specific designs outright for American production. The first to come to the Commission's attention was Marc Birkigt's Hispano-Suiza V-8 which had already been officially adopted by the French Government. Eventually, the Hisso became the closest thing there was to a standardized Allied engine. Fifty thousand were built in four countries, and they flew an assortment of planes painted with British, French, or American colors. It is not generally known that the World War I American "Jenny" was powered by Hispano engines built in America under Birkigt license.

Next to come to the American Commission's attention was a brilliant sixteen-cylinder, 500-horsepower engine designed by that enigmatic genius Ettore Bugatti. The Commission was highly impressed with the big Bugatti—which included a provision for firing a 37 MM cannon through the propeller hub—and Charles B. King of the U. S. Signal Corps was selected to oversee the project to manufacture the Bugatti in America. It was one of those classic confluences of fate that the Duesenberg Motors Corporation of Elizabeth, New Jersey, was appointed to build the Bugatti, for some of its advanced concepts were to make a distinct and significant impression upon the Duesenberg brothers and the future of their automobiles. The selection of Duesenberg also had obviously practical aspects, for the company was already building a four-cylinder, 125-horsepower aviation engine used in American training planes. Duesenberg was also active in the early activity with the "Liberty" engine, although the bulk of this project eventually went to Packard. Aircraft engine expertise gathered from these projects, the Bugatti venture, and others later permitted Duesenberg to build the most ambitious American aviation engine of all, a 900-horsepower, V-16 monster.

It is not surprising that the American Commission in Paris was impressed by the big Bugatti, even though the French themselves had not chosen to adopt it as an official design. Nevertheless, the engine must have evoked quite a few exclamations of "Formidable!" along the banks of the Seine, for it was simultaneously a monumental piece of machinery and the product of creative thinking. Although it is sometimes referred to as a V-16, that nomenclature is not correct for the design actually consisted of a pair of straight-eight engines mounted parallel to each other on a common crankcase. Bugatti had ignored Ernest Henry's double overhead-camshaft as used in the Peugeot Grand Prix cars in favor of single overhead-camshafts for each of the eight cylinder motors. The overhead camshafts operated three cams and three valves per cylinder. From one of his prototype engines Ettore Bugatti had coaxed an imposing 520 horsepower at 2200 RPM. Perhaps the American preoccupation with power even at that date had more than a little influence in the selection of Bugatti's design for execution by the Duesenbergs.

To start the project off, Bugatti sent a sample engine to Elizabeth (an eight cylinder was also purportedly sent) accompanied by his faithful number one man, Ernest Friderich, who was paid $15.00 a day by the U.S. Government for his American "tour of duty". Everyone at Elizabeth was duly awed by the French engine, not the least of whom was Fred Duesenberg who quickly recognized the land possibilities of "half" of the monster sixteen. It was almost possible to hear the wheels turning in his head.

Preliminary tests of the engine in the middle of February, 1918, however, proved somewhat disappointing. The engine began to act up on the test stand with abnormal vibration,

The Straight Eight Is Born

and when Duesenberg engineers pulled it down they found that two bearings had failed which had caused a rod and piston to disintegrate and to crack the crankcase. Friderich diplomatically reported to *le Patron* (Bugatti) that the engine had been run without an airplane propellor or any other cooling system, causing unusually high internal temperatures, and thus the oil had lost density and failed to give proper lubrication.

Tests with the Bugatti went on into the summer of 1918 under the guidance of the Duesenbergs and Charles B. King, the engineer in charge, by which time the engine was producing 460 horsepower at 2190 RPM. It was not, however, quite the same machine that Bugatti had sent over earlier that year, for King had made a number of significant design changes which were incorporated into the final Duesenberg product. Mostly, the changes were in the interests of simplifying the engine for mass production such as re-designing the front end to eliminate the very complicated double bearings used on the original French model. Similarly, King re-designed the water jacketing of the cylinder blocks and the water circulating system for more simplicity, "resulting in the elimination of many pipes and connections", as the official report put it.

But the most significant change made at Elizabeth was the substitution of a high pressure lubrication system for Bugatti's original splash system. King defended the change on the ground that the substitution was made "in conformity with the best current aeronautical engine practice and has been justified by the performance of the motor under test, and from the further fact that the original Bugatti motor failed to lubricate satisfactorily on tests in this country." From a practical point of view, the sixteen-cylinder was now much more suitable for regular production by the Duesenbergs as a result of King's design changes. But Bugatti thought otherwise. Ettore was rarely known for self-effacing modesty, and predictably

The Duesenberg

fired off a long letter to Elizabeth regretting that he had not been "warned beforehand" about the changes. However, he acknowledged the competency of the American engineers, and humbly resigned himself to an advisory capacity. He then proceeded to analyze each change in detail and to explain how his original plan was preferable! In any other man it would have been sheer pomposity, but with the world's most successful builder of racing cars anything else would have been completely out of character.

So, we have the efforts of Ettore Bugatti, Charles B. King, and Frederick and August Duesenberg pooled to produce one of the most outstanding and prophetic engines of the World War I era. Without lapsing into lengthy technical jargon, the President of Duesenberg Motors Corporation, J. R. Harbeck, summarized the project which had absorbed so much of their time and initiative in 1918. Considering the influence that these concepts were to have on the future of Duesenberg in particular and American motoring in general it seems worthwhile to take a quick look at some excerpts of what Mr. Harbeck had to say about the "twin straight-eight".

First, he pointed out that the motor consisted "substantially of two eight-cylinder motors arranged side by side"; incidentally, a technique used by Duesenberg in setting a world's record in 1920. Harbeck admired the compactness of the package, observing that, "the overall length of the motor is exceedingly short . . . . and the motor as a whole lies within the dimensions of any aviation motor of 300 horsepower. Into this concentrated package is incorporated a motor conservatively rated at 420 horsepower and actually capable of delivering 500 horsepower at approximately 1550 RPM, propellor speed."

"Carburetion and ignition are arranged in groups of four cylinders thus avoiding complicated and uneven gas distribu-

The Straight Eight Is Born

tion and difficulties in ignition incident to the ordinary six and twelve-cylinder grouping."

"This motor has probably the most substantial crankcase found in any aviation motor."

"The use of sixteen comparatively small cylinders results in a perfectly balanced running condition and perfect synchronization. The size of the cylinders permits operation with safety at high engine speed and the skilled adoption of the gear principle permits the use of these engine speeds at *useful* propellor speeds. The maximum power of the motor as developed on the stand may therefore be made useful in flight, which is *not* true of the non-geared type of motor. This condition represents the outstanding advantage of the Bugatti motor over any motor approaching it in power."

"The motor, in weight per horsepower, compares favorably with the Liberty and is much lighter per horsepower than the Rolls-Royce or other reliable foreign motors. On the base of its rated horsepower (420) the weight is two and a half pounds per horsepower, and upon the base of its maximum useful horsepower approximately *two pounds per horsepower.*"

"It may be noted that the motor as (presently) built is essentially a low compression engine, and as need develops there is every reasonable expectation of securing very much greater powers by increase in compression."

In the summer of 1918, Washington's opinion of the Bugatti-Duesenberg rose high enough to place orders for two thousand engines, which Friderich thought could be completed by June of 1919. By the Armistice, however, when production had really just begun in earnest, only about forty engines had been completed. Shortly afterward, the contracts were cancelled and no further work was done on this highly intriguing machine. What happened to most of these forty-odd Duesenberg-built Bugatti engines is obscure, although, fortunately, at least two survive today in American museums, one at the Smithsonian Institution and another at the United States Air Force Museum at Wright-Patterson AFB. In his definitive study *Bugatti—le pur sang des automobiles,* H. G. Conway mentions that the engines later served such menial but curious needs as operating "wind machines" for the movies, deflecting flames in oil well fires, and blowing air across orange groves to keep frost from forming.

Despite the little actual practical value which came from the intense Franco-American project, it may all be considered worthwhile because it served to channel Fred Duesenberg's thinking along new and exciting lines. The self-taught Iowa engineer realized that as a result of war-won technology the automobile would never be the same again and that the next few years would see vast, undreamed of improvements in motorcars. And at the head of the column Fred envisioned a powerful car driven not by four or six but by eight cylinders in a row. It became an all-encompassing thought, virtually an obsession, and it pushed his pre-war "walking beam" four-cylinder completely out of the picture.

The Duesenbergs daringly decided to subordinate everything to the eight cylinder dream; to gamble all that they had achieved from their early dirt track days. Rights to the old four-cylinder Duesenberg engine—still a popular and valuable commodity—were sold to the Rochester Motors Company and the Duesenberg engine throbbed on under the bonnets of such cars as Revere, Roamer, Kenworthy, and Meteor. Rochester Motors did not hesitate to capitalize on the "powered by Duesenberg" aspect in their advertising. If there was any doubt that the Duesenbergs were totally serious about breaking all ties with the past to concentrate on their eight-cylinder, it was

The Straight Eight Is Born

dispelled when the still new plant and equipment at Elizabeth were sold to Willys Motors.

From their voluntary liquidation, the Duesenbergs salvaged a modest amount of capital to finance their noble experiment. A room in Fred Duesenberg's house in Elizabeth was converted into a drawing office, and work was enthusiastically begun on what was to become America's first "straight eight". The design which emerged from that room showed that Fred had paid close attention to Ettore Bugatti's aero engine. The single overhead-camshaft was there (unique on an automobile on this side of the Atlantic), as well as Bugatti's three valves per cylinder with heavy emphasis laid on valve and port area for the exhaust. Duesenberg disdained Bugatti's practice of a cam for each valve, preferring to operate the exhaust valves with a rocker arm device which later proved rather unsatisfactory. Displacement was 183 cubic inches (three litres), a modest displacement but high efficiency machine which stood quite at odds with contemporary American practice, but which probably would have delighted Bugatti who had been in the vanguard of such thinking for years. In fact, it is interesting to compare the Duesenberg with Bugatti's own first straight-eight automobile. Both were single overhead-camshaft, three-valve-per-cylinder straight-eights of three-litre displacement, although Duesenberg's production model, the "A", was raised to 4.2 litres and Bugatti's production model, the Type 30, was reduced to two litres. As we shall see later, the parallel between Duesenberg and Bugatti thinking and development with the straight eight concept would similarly culminate in unique, high-performance, luxury machines.

Not surprisingly, the first straight eights were destined for the Duesenbergs' first love—racing. They were ready for the first postwar edition of the Indianapolis 500 in 1919, but apparently teething troubles forestalled any victory celebrations for that maiden outing. Next year, however, Duesenberg made a strong showing in the classic race with third, fourth, and sixth places. And it was just the beginning. The early Twenties were to be exciting times for Duesenberg on both road and track.

3

The Model "A"

The Sixteenth Automobile Salon held at the Commodore Hotel in New York in November of 1920 marked a milestone in automotive history. For the first time, Americans could look at— and order—an American car which had entered much the same circle of sophistication as the grand marques of Europe such as Hispano-Suiza, Mercedes, Rolls-Royce, or Isotta Fraschini. In the early history of the automobile, America's chief contribution had been the miracle of mass production rather than technical innovation; and when the well-heeled customer went shopping for a carriage *de grand luxe* he frequently ended with an import. Trends were set by people like William K. Vanderbilt who kept a stable well filled with Mercedes cars painted in German racing white and Rolls-Royces finished in the Vanderbilt's own maroon coaching color.

The new Duesenberg "Straight Eight" which made its debut that November was an alluring alternative. It offered an effective challenge to the view that nothing technically interesting originated on this side of the Atlantic, for the first Duesenberg passenger car offered for public sale had plenty in the way of novel engineering. It was an uncannily accurate prediction of what fine cars would be like a decade or more later.

The first Duesenberg touring car which sat ostentatiously alone in the foyer at the Commodore Hotel had made it there by the skin of its teeth; it was a last-minute entry without advance reservation and Fred Duesenberg had to bribe the hotel people to clear a space for it. The unique showpiece (it was the only Duesenberg tourer in existence at the time) had been rushed up from Elizabeth the day before with Fred Duesenberg's Buick running along behind laden with show materials and publicity handouts. It was a lucky move, for the Duesenberg—symbolically segregated from its competitors—attracted a lion's share of attention. Fully half of the people who picked up advertising material returned postcards requesting further details.

Curiously, there is some evidence that the actual showcar was something of a "mechanical mutation" because it was neither a derivative of its race bred brothers nor a close prototype of the actual production version of the model which it represented. Apparently, the boys were still feeling their way at this point, making the transition from racing to commercial practice. The November 25, 1920 issue of *Motor Age* had this to say on the subject: "In the engine shown at the Salon, the well known Duesenberg arrangement of valves is used, the inlet and exhaust valves being arranged in the cylinder head horizontally and operated by means of rocker levers extending up the sides of the cylinders. However, owing to the very satisfactory results obtained with the racing engines, which have inclined valves in the head, operated by an overhead camshaft, it has been decided to adopt this construction in the stock cars, and this feature will be introduced in the next lot of engines to be built."

The Duesenbergs did not soft pedal their first passenger car. The introduction announcements which they handed out at the Salon forthrightly proclaimed that the Duesenberg **Straight**

Fred Duesenberg with the first born. This is the No. 1 Model A Duesenberg that sat in the foyer of the Commodore Hotel and singlehandedly caused a sensation at the Sixteenth Automobile Salon in November, 1920. (*Photo, Wm. C. Kinsman*)

Eight was "Built to outclass, out-run, and out-last any car on the road." The advertising flyer identified the car as being "Exhibited by (the) Duesenberg Brothers, To Be Built by the Duesenberg Automobile and Motors Company, Inc., Indianapolis, Indiana."

The new company had set up virtually at the Indianapolis Speedway's main gate (actually two miles away) in what was then the heart land of the American motor industry. Transfer of operations from Elizabeth to Indiana began not long after the close of the Salon, and the new plant officially opened on June 1st, 1921. It was here that the "next lot of engines" mentioned by *Motor Age* was begun. And it was here that life was

The second example of the Model A, handbuilt at Elizabeth, New Jersey, just before the factory was moved to Indianapolis. (*Photo, Wm. C. Kinsman*)

first breathed into the car which later came to be called the "Model A" Duesenberg. The new factory's inaugural effort was the building of a batch of eight chassis (what Rolls-Royce endearingly calls a "sanction" of chassis) which really were the first true "A"s.

The "Model A" was something which is rarely encountered today; virtually a wholly new car conceived and created from the ground up. At its heart lay the most radical production engine ever put into an American car up to that time. The "A" engine was scaled up from the racing engine's three litres to 4.2 litres (260 cubic inches)—racing engines were getting

The Model A

smaller and faster—but the single overhead-camshaft was retained, although the racing practice of three valves per cylinder was dropped to a more conventional pair of valves for each cylinder. On this *Motor Age* commented: "While in the racing engine two exhaust valves and one inlet valve are used per cylinder, the passenger car engine will have only a single inlet and a single exhause valve." Also, it might be noted here that, according to *Motor Age,* "This change in the design will make it possible to completely machine the compression chambers, the advantage of which is that it permits of making all eight compression chambers of exactly equal volume, which tends to promote smooth running, and to prevent the adherence of carbon deposits to the combustion chamber walls."

Curiously, especially since it was an eight-cylinder engine, the Duesenberg crankshaft rode in a scanty three main bearings, although in practice everything seemed very sturdy and quite vibration free owing to a very carefully thought out system of counterweights. As in the revised Bugatti aero engine a pressure lubrication system was used. The Duesenbergs favored aluminum alloy pistons in their engines, having generally used them with success in their racing engines. But there seemed at the time to be something of a public prejudice against aluminum pistons, so Duesenberg offered "A" customers a choice of either aluminum or cast iron pistons.

In summary, the Duesenberg "A" engine represented a high point of smooth running, efficient power; putting out eighty eight horsepower at 3600 RPM and offering speeds of 100 MPH plus. Obviously, to have placed such an advanced engine in a conventional chassis would have been near sacrilege. But here Duesenberg chassis expertise proved equal to the challenge—and then some! The most notable feature of the "A" chassis was its premier American use of four-wheel brakes. It is worthwhile to point out here that the early cars were generally much more successful at going than at stopping. The

The Duesenberg

1903 "Sixty" Mercedes began to pay some attention to braking by providing an early water cooling system for the brake drums, and by 1909 Isotta-Fraschini of Italy had fitted the world's first four-wheel brakes as standard equipment on a production car. Peugeot used four-wheel brakes to some advantage in the 1914 French Grand Prix, although the benefit was not enough to win. A major advance in brakes came in 1919 with Marc Birkigt's application of his brilliant servo-mechanism braking, which Rolls-Royce adopted and used in modified form all the way up to the 1966 Silver Shadow, which went over to discs. Yet, even well into the 1920s four-wheel brakes remained a novelty and in America Duesenberg's four-wheel hydraulic brakes were totally unique.

Fred Duesenberg's hydraulic braking system, which descended from his 1914 racing machine, operated in a manner not unfamiliar to modern drivers. When the brake pedal was depressed it engaged a piston in the master cylinder which began to pump the hydraulic brake fluid out of the master cylinder chamber and into the brake lines. In accordance with Duesenberg's frequent philosophy of a "back up" system for everything possible, there was a second or "booster piston" which fed in extra fluid and increased the pressure to supplement the master cylinder, resulting in a brake line pressure of up to five hundred pounds. The hydraulic pressure which carried through the special lines operated smaller cylinders in each of the four wheels which transmitted the pressure of the driver's foot on the brake pedal to expand the brake shoes

Thanks to Fred Duesenberg's four-wheel hydraulic brakes this Model A could stop with uncommon certainty. Fine brakes plus the many other refinements on the A eventually ran the chassis price up to $8300, the second most expensive car in America at the time. Shown is a four-passenger touring body by Fleetwood. (*Photo, Wm. C. Kinsman*)

Some historians lay the demise of the Model A to its overly conservative body designs which give little impression of the modern and very willing chassis below. (*Photo, Wm. C. Kinsman*)

against the sixteen-inch finned drums. To summarize, it was a superb method of stopping, quite equal to the Duesenberg's inclination to go. It was also a system quite characteristic of Fred Duesenberg, even down to his failure to patent it!

One continued to uncover Duesenberg unorthodoxy as he examined the chassis of the new Straight Eight; discovering such novelties as tubular front axles, a torque tube incorporated as a unit assembly with the back axle, and, a bit later, even the first balloon tires used on an American passenger car. Together, the engine and chassis of the new Duesenberg represented an epochal collection of "firsts" in a single car. For such enlightened progress, one paid well; the Straight Eight

Formal elegance on the Model A Duesenberg chassis, an imposing town Brougham by Fleetwood. (*Photo, Wm. C. Kinsman*)

Stamina and durability were built into the Model A. In 1923 an A did a simulated trans-continental run of 3155 miles in about 50 hours at an average speed of 63 MPH. Shown here, a Fleetwood roadster. (*Photo, Wm. C. Kinsman*)

Duesenberg was the second most expensive car built in America at the time, up to $8300 by the time it was succeeded by the "J". Only the potent Doble steam car commanded a higher price ($11,800), at best a temporary glory for the steamer.

For all those one hundred-cent dollars the affluent Duesenberg customer of the twenties got his money's worth. He got a car that was as honestly and solidly built as the hand of man could make it, and he got a car that seemed to go on running forever—fast. To demonstrate their car's unique stamina Duesenberg devised a spectacular non-stop "coast to coast" run of over three thousand miles to be held in full view on the Indianapolis Speedway. In the spring of 1923, a standard production Duesenberg touring car appeared on the Indy bricks. Its driver started the engine, went through the gears, and

Model A Duesenberg with a Fleetwood touring body. The A Engine was scaled up from the three-litre racing engine to 4.2 litres (260 cubic inches) and could put out 88 HP at 3600 RPM. (*Photo, Wm. C. Kinsman*)

A unique car which provided a hint of things to come; the Model X Duesenberg boat-tail speedster with all-aluminum body. (*Photo, Wm. C. Kinsman*)

settled down to a brisk clip which he couldn't have duplicated on the roads of the 1920s between New York and Los Angeles. Hour after hour the car droned on. Every now and then another Duesenberg would pull up alongside—at speeds of up to ninety miles an hour—to supply fuel, water, and relief drivers. Even a spark plug was changed at speed. The car had to stop twice for tires, but the motor got no respite.

A little over fifty hours later the Duesenberg completed the simulated 3155 miles trans-continental run with an average speed of nearly 63 MPH. It was the most spectacular showing of automotive reliability since a Silver Ghost Rolls-Royce ran the celebrated Scottish Reliability Trial and endurance run in

The rare and mysterious Model X Duesenberg represented the factory's concept of an "all new" Duesenberg for 1927. This racy dual-cowl phaeton suggests a definite break with the dowdy earlier Model A and accurately predicts the feeling of the Model J which was still nearly two years away. (*Photo, Wm. C. Kinsman*)

1907 and covered 15,000 trouble-free miles. In another showing, a Duesenberg was loosed on the Indianapolis Speedway and continued to circumnavigate the track for three full weeks, covering over 18,000 miles.

Such demonstrations, combined with Duesenberg's great victory in the 1921 French Grand Prix, were convincing sales pitches for the marque, and Duesenberg ads dropped lines like "The most consistent performance of any automobile manufactured", and "The Grand Prix car". From a purely logical viewpoint, the Duesenberg had every chance for success; a brilliantly designed, well made, and highly reliable car introduced into an affluent, free and easy age which was having a rollicking love affair with the automobile.

While the Duesenberg "Model A" did not quite fall flat on its face as some observers have suggested, it is quite accurate to say that there was considerable variance between its engine power curve and the upward trend of the black lines on its sales charts. Considering what they were being offered, Americans did a notably effective job of ignoring the best car their country had to offer. In 1922 when production facilities were pretty well established only ninety two cars were sold. The following year, the Model A's best sales record was reached, 140 units. Although the car was hardly conceived to move over the counter like Model T Fords or Volkswagens, these figures do seem unduly modest even by unhurried European measurement.

If a modern Madison Avenue market analyst were to investigate why people stayed away from Duesenberg salesrooms in droves, it would probably not take him long to point his finger and say "Packaging". In many of the "A" models, particularly the earlier specimens, there was little to suggest the avant garde thinking which lay concealed beneath the well built but stoic and staid coachwork. Born into an age remembered for its bacchanalian love of the good life, the new

Shades of the Roaring Twenties; a Duesenberg Straight Eight waits in front of the police station at Auburn.

Duesenberg often offered a sharply contrasting image of stolid conservatism. Despite their high quality, many Duesenbergs of the early twenties were the antithesis of racy Bugattis, menacing Mercedes, or suave Hispano-Suizas. It was a sad circumstance that the "Model A" was a sartorial miscalculation; an unfortunate mismatch of superb chassis with undistinguished coachwork. It was something like putting a Ferrari chassis under a black Volkswagon body and then wondering what happened to the carriage trade.

Eventually, however, Duesenberg learned the truism that "the package sells the product", and the stodgy "A" finally metamorphosed into the Monarch. Toward the end of the "A's" reign some extremely striking dual cowl phaetons appeared which were reliable prophecies of what was to come in the next great epoch of the Duesenberg story. The racier look of

31

the later "A" models may have been a reflection of some forward thinking which was going on at Indianapolis to create an "all new" Duesenberg for 1927. The results of this thinking culminated in a somewhat mysterious machine which has come to be called the "Model X" Duesenberg. (Authors' Note: Both "Model A" and "Model X" were not contemporary factory nomenclature, but designations added later to differentiate the earlier cars from the later J and SJ models.) The successor car differed in a number of chassis changes, including stretching the wheelbase one inch to 135 inches, and increasing the horsepower output from 88 to 100 HP.

The "X", which basically represented a further polishing and perfection of the concepts of the "A" (and a last attempt to capture the public fancy), was a rare breed. Only a dozen were built and these few cars represented the zenith of Duesenberg mastery of the automotive arts in 1927.

The times were tenuous for Duesenberg. The "A" was now shelved after a production run of what Duesenberg historian Raymond A. Wolff estimates to be about five hundred cars, of which about one in five still survives. For all its high devotion to duty, the Duesenberg enterprise was gradually being inundated by red ink. Had it not been for the intervention of a modern Don Quixote by the name of Erret Lobban Cord it would probably have soon submerged.

Cord had the highest appreciation of Duesenberg's talents. "I have observed one outstanding engineering genius and that is Fred S. Duesenberg", he said upon purchasing the company which had fallen into receivership by the latter part of 1926. Yet Cord the gallant, visored knight (see the Cord "coat of arms") on horseback did not ride to the rescue on purely altruistic motives. Cord was an anomaly in the industry, a dynamic young businessman who dared to shake the automobile business by the tail and was lucky enough to land in the driver's seat. Cord was as aware as any of today's manufac-

The Model A

turers—of soap or automobiles—that packaging sells the product. In 1924, he acquired the flagging Auburn company, gave the car a dramatic facelifting, and amazed the discouraged stockholders by mailing them dividend checks. From then on he could do no wrong, including such a bold move as buying the Duesenberg enterprise.

With the self-sure certainty of a computer, Cord knew what the American public wanted in a super luxury car, and he was confident that Duesenberg was the only organization which could supply it. When he acquired the Duesenberg interests at Indianapolis, Cord announced that his "purchase of the Duesenberg factory is the culmination of my plans to offer the world an automobile of undisputed rank—in fact, the finest thing on four wheels." It was a well turned phrase, and it turned out to be considerably more than a copy writer's quip.

4

The Mighty Model "J"

When the first Duesenberg Model J was exhibited—still not entirely completed—at the 1928 New York Salon, Messrs. Cord and Duesenberg were very sure of themselves . . . so sure, in fact, that the truly revolutionary car carried no nameplate, an act of self-effacing anonymity to outstrip even the conservatism of Rolls-Royce! According to the catalogue, "The superlatively fine has no need to be boastful. So confident is Duesenberg of the unquestioned supreme position that its product occupies that a nameplate is considered superfluous. Nowhere on the car will you find the name Duesenberg." However, the company later had second thoughts about this and added the Duesenberg eagle motif with the words "Duesenberg Straight Eight" to the radiator grille and firewall.

Insignia aside, Cord and the Duesenberg brothers had good reason to be confident and proud of the new creation. The advertising writer's claim of "the world's finest motor car" was not without substance, and in the next few years many satisfied buyers came to accept that statement as literal truth.

Erret Lobban Cord knew exactly what he wanted in a super luxury car and, even more significantly, he understood perhaps

The Mighty Model "J"

better than any other man the workings of the industry which produced automobiles as well as the workings of the minds of the people who bought them. As a bright-eyed teenager, Cord's original investment in the automobile business was $75.00 paid to a Los Angeles used car dealer for a rusty relic which vaguely resembled an automobile. A few weeks later, the car emerged from the Cord backyard with a new body, a re-built engine (well warmed up in the process), and bright red wire wheels. From the day Cord sold his restored car for $675 he never looked back. He promptly repeated the process, this time for $1200, and within a year twenty cars had passed through his hands, each leaving him with a $500 profit.

From there he worked his way through a series of auto dealerships from California to Chicago, where the duties included sweeping floors, pumping gas, and squirting grease as well as selling cars. Eventually, there was a partnership in a Chicago agency which grew and prospered under Cord's hand. Then he heard about Auburn. Cord came to the Auburn company in the summer of 1924 and found it at disaster's door, ranking thirty-fourth in sales among American automobile builders and dead last in morale. Three months later the heavily indebted company owed no one a penny and had $150,000 in the bank. A year later it had risen to fourteenth place in sales, was selling two million dollars worth of automobiles a month, and had earned a net profit of $800,000. Erret Lobban Cord was a man well worth listening to; when he proposed to buy another endangered auto manufacturer named Duesenberg, and even when he went so far as to tell Fred Duesenberg how to build an automobile!

Cord was notably dissatisfied with the Model X Duesenberg as a base from which to carry out his grand plans for Duesenberg. As we have seen, the Model X was the focus of activity at Indianapolis when Cord took over in October of 1926. He permitted the car to be developed to its conclusion and a few

Rear compartment of the Le Grande Torpedo Phaeton, for passengers who liked to keep informed. (*Photo, Wm. C. Kinsman*)

production models were made. In proposing his plans to Duesenberg for his "dream car", Cord found that Fred Duesenberg had a few ideas of his own. As a conservative luxury car, the Model A and its successor had not been a resounding commercial success, although the sporty phaetons had evoked much public interest. Perhaps Fred Duesenberg was reasoning that it might be best to leave the luxury market to others and concentrate on a lithe and sporty high-performance, high-efficiency car to appeal to the young at heart. Perhaps Duesenberg was looking closely at the glory and gains that were going

The dual-cowl Torpedo Phaeton with body by Weyman-Le Grande. Disc wheels had come into vogue by this time and replaced the racy open wires on this car. (*Photo, Wm. C. Kinsman*)

The "Riviera Phaeton", a four door convertible sedan with the convenience of roll-up windows in the doors to replace the old-fashioned side curtains. The design was created by J. Herbert Newport as a show car for the 1934 season. Later, Colonel Schick, the electric razor magnate, bought one.

to Bugatti in France and Bentley in Britain, both of whom were more concerned in the middle twenties with sports machinery than grand luxury cars. Whatever the reasoning, there is some indication that at this stage Fred Duesenberg had considered turning his hand to a small, high-efficiency sporting machine.

A very early example of the SJ, a Le Grande dual-cowl phaeton with no less than Fred Duesenberg in command. Note the one-piece exhaust manifold which was later replaced with the more familiar jointed four external exhausts. (*Photo, Wm. C. Kinsman*)

The heart of the matter; the magnificent piece of steel sculpture that was the great Duesenberg J powerplant. Duesenberg's underhood layout was one of the most elegant in the history of motorcars; a mailed fist in a velvet glove. (*Photo, Wm. C. Kinsman*)

E. L. Cord replied with a flat "no" to any suggestion for a sporty smaller car. Cannily, he sensed the American indifference to fine sports cars and projected that a Duesenberg sports car would be a repeat of the Model A, an undoubtedly fine car that would be much admired but which probably would not sell in sufficient numbers to support itself. Cord was quite correct in his analysis, as a brief glance at the unfortunate history of the Stutz will illustrate—a fine American sports car probably more appreciated in Europe than at home. In spite

Installing the great seven-litre double overhead-camshaft engines in chassis. (*Photo, Wm. C. Kinsman*)

of the fact that America was statistically the most motor-minded nation on earth, a relatively small percentage of Americans was genuinely devoted to automobiles and knew them as intimately as Europeans, a condition which largely still persists. In his book, *Kings of the Road,* Ken Purdy spends a chapter on "The Hallowed Bricks of Indianapolis" and reaches the inevitable conclusion that the annual May migration to Indianapolis—then and now—is more a demonstration in mass psychology than a measure of American appreciation of fine machinery.

The finished product at Indianapolis; a row of J chassis awaiting attention by custom coachbuilders. (*Photo, Wm. C. Kinsman*)

Cord, being more a realist than a romanticist, preferred to leave the negligible American sports car market of the 1920s to the importers or to whomever would cater to it. Cord's analysis of what the affluent American wanted in a car was exceptionally shrewd, and quite typical of him. The "Age of Aquarius" has nothing on the 1920s. Daring young men were flying to Paris instead of to the moon, welcome new social freedoms were emerging, then as now there were alluringly illegal intoxicants to be trifled with, and showrooms were filled with shiny new cars and happy people with shiny new money. It was a scene that brooked nothing small, and generously rewarded those who "thought big". E. L. Cord realized that "good" and "big" were virtually synonymous words in the American vo-

The Mighty Model "J"

cabulary, and inevitably that the American measure of an automobile was (and still is) reduced to "How much does it cost?" and "How fast will it go?". Stated simply, Cord envisioned a car which would be bigger, faster, more expensive —and, incidentally, better —than any other car. Thus was born the Model J Duesenberg which would fulfill all of Cord's prophecies, including the ability to make money for its builders.

The idea for the Model J Duesenberg fitted in with Cord's often quoted philosophy, "If you can't be biggest, it pays to be different." The Duesenberg plant at Indianapolis was certainly not the biggest. There was a relatively modest two story office building separated by a court yard from an unimposing factory building which really didn't look much like the birthplace of "The finest thing on four wheels". In all, about fifty

It was the Duesenberg philosophy to test each chassis individually before it left the factory. Here, seven J8s waiting in line for proving at the Indianapolis Speedway. (*Photo, Wm. C. Kinsman*)

Hedgerows, Tudor respectability, and a Rollston convertible victoria; coachwork design by Gordon Buehrig, interior design by J. Herbert Newport. (*Photo, Wm. C. Kinsman*)

people worked in both buildings. Cord's idea of being different —to leap ahead of his competitors by a country mile—was not novel, but his success in achieving it is virtually unique in American industrial history. However, all the commercial philosophy, the talk of biggest and best, and the grandiose leaping ahead of competitors would have been so many words

This Walker roadster featured an early semi-automatic top. Note the small hole in the rear panel just behind the door hinges in which a crank could be inserted to raise and lower the top. (*Photo, Wm. C. Kinsman*)

The Duesenberg

and drawings on paper had it not been for the technical genius of Fred Duesenberg. If there was ever a perfect "marriage of convenience" it was the association of the Brothers Duesenberg and Erret Lobban Cord.

So, it was this interplay of talent, money, and foresight which brought the Duesenberg to the floor of the 1928 New York salon. As his prospective clients gathered around to "oh", "ah", and otherwise pay homage, perhaps the thought crossed Cord's mind that in his enthusiasm maybe he had overdone it. Maybe the Duesenberg was just *too* much of everything; a shade past that barrier which separates the merely "larger than life" from the preposterous. But no, Cord had guessed just right; the Duesenberg symbolized the gilded age of American cars the way Versailles symbolized the age of *le roi soleil*.

To describe what Duesenberg and Cord had conspired to create is not a simple thing. Some people are primarily enchanted with the lush and lovely coachwork which clothed the Duesenberg chassis. Others stress the singular engineering achievement which Fred Duesenberg laid underneath the sheet metal and hand rubbed lacquer. Although detailed technical descriptions generally do not impart much of the true flavor of a car as an entirety, an account of the "workings" of the Duesenberg engine and chassis is perhaps the best place to start, as well as being a good example of the Duesenberg

A case of "the customer is right but the designer knows best". A great amount of thought and attention to detail went into this unusual Duesenberg built by Wolfington, a half-century-old Philadelphia coachbuilder. The emphasis was on comfort and the owner's personal taste. Concealed radio aerials are nothing new; this car had the aerial interwoven between the top and top lining, specially arranged so that the top could be folded without damaging the aerial wires. J. Herbert Newport designed the car, but the distracting moulding effect was the owner's own fling at body design. (*Photo, Wm. C. Kinsman*)

way of doing things. For those more impressed with the visual aspects of Duesenbergs we have reserved the next chapter.

Besides the general description and heady coachwork illustrations, the Duesenberg catalogue disassembled the chassis and engine into its basic components and discussed (and pictured) each part with delicate care. To the society matron perusing the town cars, it was so much wasted space, but to the sporting gentleman contemplating the rakish roadsters and phaetons it was pure manna. First, there was the fully astonishing engine which Fred Duesenberg had created to power Cord's concept of the biggest, fastest, and most powerful car of them all. It was, of course, a great straight eight, displacing 6.9 liters (420 cubic inches) with a bore and stroke of 95 MM × 121 MM (3¾ × 4¾ inches). In an age accustomed to mammoth displacement the Duesenberg engine was big, but not startlingly so (the New Phantom Rolls-Royce went to 470 cubic inches). Yet, the bare statistics did not even hint at the rampant power which was on tap.

For maximum efficiency and power extraction, Duesenberg went over from the single overhead-camshaft of the Model A to a double overhead-cam arrangement, which of course had been the hallmark of the all-out racing machine since Ernest Henry had first used it in the futuristic Peugeot Grand Prix car of 1912. The Duesenberg double overhead-camshafts operated an amazing *four* valves per cylinder, something unique in passenger cars. Even the successful 1921 French Grand Prix winning Duesenberg racing car had used only three valves per cylinder. The valves were of silichrome steel, and reputedly required adjustment only once every ten thousand miles. Although the Duesenberg, like the Hispano-Suiza, never made

The cream of classics; a Le Grande "swept panel" Duesenberg dual cowl phaeton on the 142½-inch wheelbase. (*Photo, Wm. C. Kinsman*)

Ultimate elegance in the formal mood—Duesenberg J town car. (*Photo, Gladding Rolls-Royce, Inc.*)

much claim to the Rolls-Royce type of silent operation, the inevitable clatter of thirty-two valves was still rather effectively suppressed by cutting "quieting ramps" in the cams and by immersing the cams completely in oil. The fully machined combustion chambers were designed for maximum efficiency, nearly hemispherical in shape with the spark plug centered for short flame travel, and everything was very generously surrounded by water jacketing.

The Duesenberg catalogue called its heat treated aluminum alloy connecting rods "the best ever made", and explained that "Duesenberg pistons are unique". The pistons were, in fact, quite novel and worthy of mention. They were of a

Style and speed in the grand manner; a convertible J roadster designed by J. Herbert Newport and built by Walker-Le Grande. (*Photo, Wm. C. Kinsman*)

Walter M. Murphy Company, Coachbuilders of Pasadena, is closely identified with Duesenberg, having built more bodies for Duesenberg chassis than any other builder. Here, a Murphy phaeton touring design on a J chassis for a sporty yet conservative look. (*Photo, Wm. C. Kinsman*)

hardened aluminum alloy and constructed with a split skirt attached to the head which was designed to expand and contract at precisely the same rate as the cylinder bore, so that the pistons always fit the bore perfectly in either a hot or cold engine. Three compression rings and one oil ring were used.

A popular interpretation on the Duesenberg chassis, and about the most economical, a Murphy convertible roadster with rumble seat. (*Photo, Wm. C. Kinsman*)

and the normal compression was modest at 5.2 to 1 but could be raised with special domed pistons.

Duesenberg's massive and imposing 150-pound, double-heat-treated, chrome-nickle steel crankshaft was an elegant piece of metal sculpture. And the way it performed its function was just as elegant as its form. Although there were only five main bearings (but 2¾ inches in diameter), a splendid smoothness was achieved through dynamically balancing the crankshaft and using a system of scientifically devised counterweights, which also served to reduce bearing pressures to add to longevity. But the most intriguing concession to smoothness has became another Duesenberg legend: the mercury vibration damper. Two containers with copper baffles inside were attached to the crankshaft just between number one and number two cylinders and were ninety four percent filled with mercury. Any stray vibrations from the engine were effectively absorbed by the "sloshing" of the mercury against the baffles. Another typical example of the Duesenberg devotion to detail. Again typical was the quadruple fuel pumping system—three electrics plus one mechanical—to ensure sufficient sustenance for the 6.9 litres from the twenty six gallon tank.

Even as it lay cool and motionless the Duesenberg "J" engine was a thing of beauty to behold. Along with the Hispano-Suiza's pressure enameled engine and that of some of the Bugattis, the underhood architecture of the Duesenberg is among the most elegant in the history of motordom. Computers are used more and more in the design of modern cars. And it is nowhere more evident than in the engine compartment of Detroit's newest gems—a cold and total devotion to

Celebrities and Duesenbergs were a natural combination. Here, Joe E. Brown and Darryl F. Zanuck, Jr. share a Duesenberg running board for a relaxed moment on a movie lot. (*Photo, Wm. C. Kinsman*)

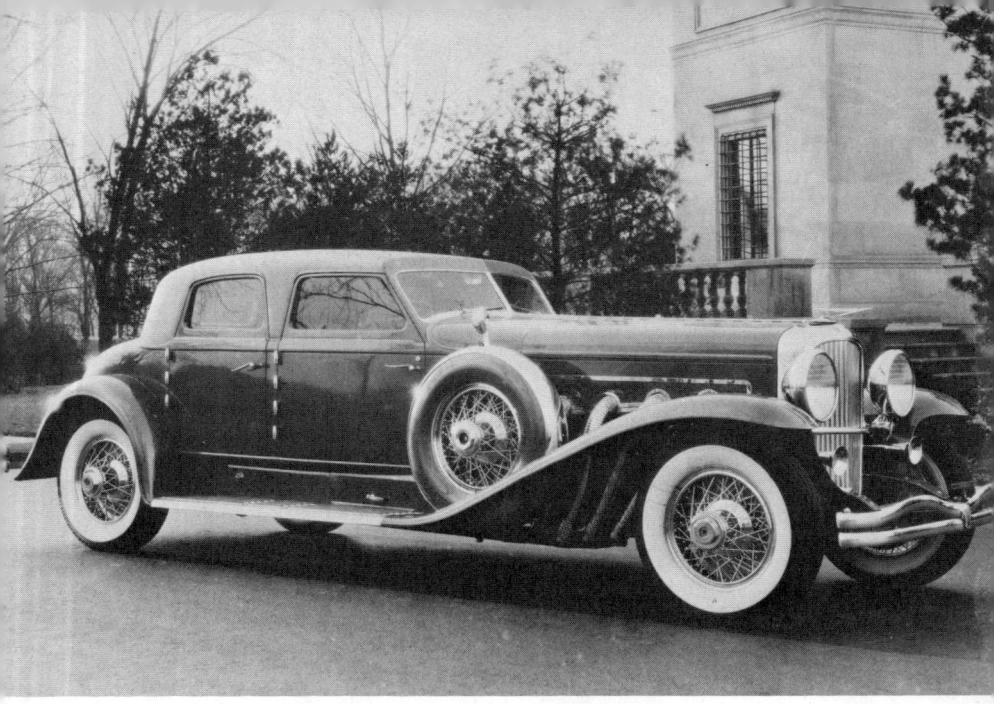

A very famous Duesenberg, the Rollston-built "Twenty Grand" SJ sedan, so called for its reported $20,000 price. (*Photo, Wm. C. Kinsman*)

doing the least at the lowest price without the slightest concession to the eye. Beneath the long Duesenberg bonnet lay a sharp contrast to the "computer cars" of today, a deliberately impressive and artistic array of aluminum, alloys, and glistening green enamel. There was heavy emphasis on sparkling metal in the Duesenberg engine room, from the long, alloy twin cam covers to the polished aluminum firewall decorated with the golden Duesenberg eagle. Duesenberg hoods were long—sometimes half the length of the car—but the roomy engine compartment was always well filled.

The underhood elegance was certainly not there to compensate for any lack of muscle—it was simply a good example of the mailed fist in a velvet glove. And that fist packed quite a

Understated elegance of the interior decor of the "Twenty Grand" Duesenberg sedan by Rollston. (*Photo, Wm. C. Kinsman*)

wallop: 265 horsepower at 4250 RPM, an astonishing turnover for a seven-litre engine in 1928. By comparison, Marc Birkigt's superb aircraft-inspired Hispano-Suiza 37.2 (six cylinders, 6.6 litres) peaked at fully a thousand revolutions less, although the Hisso did give fine low speed torque and developed 120 of its 135 horsepower at under 2000 RPM. The new Duesenberg J easily outdistanced all domestic competition at a gait. It had well over *double* the horsepower of its nearest rival, the L–80 Imperial Chrysler whose favorite claim of "America's most powerful motor car" left egg on its face. With 89 MPH

The Mighty Model "J"

available in second gear, the J could outrun any other American car on the road, with the possible exception of the Black Hawk Stutz sports, without even bothering to drop into top gear. The 116 MPH available at the top ranges of performance was fully in the stratosphere, wholly undreamed of for a three-ton luxury machine.

Despite its size and weight the J had all the verve and vitality of a prima donna sports car. No unduly long straights were required to build up speed; 100 MPH could be had exactly twenty one seconds after you pressed your foot to the floor. And the amazing thing was not so much that Fred Duesenberg could produce such prodigious performance, but that he could do it with such ease and absence of strain. The Duesenberg catalogue pointed out that a lesser car driven at very nearly its potential worked very hard, "like a runner out of breath". A Duesenberg, on the other hand, had such a surfeit of power that it could jog along while others were panting and perspiring. "With a rear axle ratio of 3.5 to 1 the engine develops 165 horsepower at 60 MPH. Only sixty horsepower is required to drive the car at this rate on a level road, leaving 105 horsepower in reserve for acceleration, hillclimbing, or both, available the instant the throttle is opened. At a mile a minute, therefore, the throttle is more than half closed with the engine producing only 37% of the power in it. Thus lightly loaded, it must give long life and freedom from trouble."

At about the same time that E. L. Cord acquired Duesenberg he also purchased Lycoming Motors of Williamsport, Pennsylvania, which did the actual construction of the J engine precisely to Fred Duesenberg's design and specifications. In all, Lycoming supplied 480 engines, and when the last bolt was

A prize from the 1930s; Gary Cooper's magnificent Derham Tourster built on the 153.5-inch-wheelbase chassis. Radiator mascot was strictly "non-issue". (*Photo, Wm. C. Kinsman*)

The Duesenberg

turned on the last engine a unique era in American automotive history ended, because, even though the Duesenberg engine was designed well over forty years ago, there is today not a single engine half so sophisticated offered by any domestic manufacturer of luxury cars. And even if there were, at today's costs such an engine would cost nearly as much as Americans are accustomed to paying for a complete car. More than a generation after the advent of the J the 1970 8.2-litre Cadillac demonstrates that Detroit still favors displacement over design.

The Lycoming-built engines were shipped to Indianapolis where they were mated with the Duesenberg chassis, which was the perfect companion to the brilliant engine. It was Fred Duesenberg's theory that the instability of a car at speed was traceable to a non-rigid frame, so he built the J frame to be extremely rigid under all circumstances this side of outright cataclysm. Accordingly, Duesenberg struck off steel work of proportions usually reserved for locomotive yards. Alloy steel 7/32 inch thick was selected for the massive frame which sank eight and a half inches deep at the center. This ladder-type frame was then braced with six cross members, the middle member consisting of a four-inch-square steel tube "riveted and welded into the frame with 8½ ×·12 inch double gussets". The second member was fitted with twenty-four-inch-long diagonal braces to provide "A" pattern bracing which gave extreme rigidity and security to the front end. For safety, the final two members (2½-inch-diameter steel tubing) surrounded the gas tank.

Perhaps the ultimate Duesenberg touring car, the legendary Torpedo Phaeton. Note early type exhaust manifold. Later, when the company offered to replace this with the newer style jointed exhausts the owner refused, saying that he liked to see it glow at night after a brisk drive. (*Photo, Wm. C. Kinsman*)

The Mighty Model "J"

All of this steel flying over the road at a mile a minute or better could be brought to an efficient halt with Duesenberg's four-wheel hydraulic brakes which represented a further development of the already advanced braking system used on the Model A. Later, a system of variable power-assisted brakes was added and won much praise. The Duesenberg brakes operated with forged steel finned drums fifteen inches in diameter and three inches wide with cast aluminum brake shoes. The magnificent chrome plated wire wheels were originally nineteen inches, later reduced to seventeen inches after 1935.

The Duesenberg driver was by far the best informed on the road about what was going on under the hood. His collection of dials and gauges which stared back at him from the dash resembled the flight deck of the Graf Zeppelin and conveyed total information about the condition of his car. Besides a 150-MPH speedometer and a 5000-RPM tachometer there was an eight-day clock with a split second hand to give "stop watch readings from ⅕ second to 30 minutes", which was a nice convenience to the performance minded driver who wanted to know exactly what times he was setting up either quarter-mile or cross country. And for the fellow who wanted to know, literally, how high he was from the exhilaration of driving a Duesenberg there was even an altimeter to give the above-sealevel altitude at a glance. More conventional instruments included a gas gauge, oil pressure gauge, engine heat indicator, and—that welcome dial—an ammeter in lieu of "charge-discharge" lights. All instruments originally had white lettering on black dials, although later the reverse pattern became available.

Some other, quite unconventional, lights also winked back

Subdued sport; the Weyman "St. Cloud" sport sedan used a super light-weight fabric body which meant even greater performance on the powerful J chassis. (*Photo, Wm. C. Kinsman*)

at the Duesenberg driver from the oxidized engine-turned nickle dash. On both sides of the dash there was a pair of vertically mounted lights. The upper light on the right side glowed red every seven hundred miles to remind the driver that a six quart oil change was required. Underneath, another light went on at 1400 miles to suggest that the battery be checked for water. A duplicate set of lights on the driver's side was connected to a primeval computer called "the timing box" and advised the driver about the Bijur automatic chassis lubricating mechanism. Inside this box a gear revolved once each eighty miles and activated a plunger which sent oil to the spring bolt bushings, drag link, shock absorber linkage, rear universal, clutch throw-out bearing, and drive shaft bearing. As long as the oil reservoir was filled the red light glowed and the green one came on to recommend a refill. The Bijur system was a convenient and practical approach to chassis lubrication; variants of the system continued in use on some Rolls-Royce and Mercedes-Benz cars until the late 1950s. Despite all the complexity of Duesenberg instrumentation, it was not unheard of for some customers to order a duplicate set of instruments in the rear passenger compartment to keep a chauffeured owner fully informed!

There was little about a Duesenberg that was conventional. Even down to something as prosaic as a muffler Duesenberg rose to the extraordinary. The Duesenberg muffler was an imposing piece of custom construction to accommodate the big, hot engine—seven inches in diameter and fifty two inches long! At different periods of construction both steel and solid copper exhaust pipes were used.

Duesenberg made extensive use of alloys to keep the chassis weight to—considering the ponderous size—a surprisingly light 4450-pound average, depending on whether the standard 142½ inch wheelbase chassis or the 153½ long wheelbase chassis was selected. For instance, despite the cost, lightweight aluminum

A choice piece of Duesenberg exotica—the Weyman-built "Fishtail" SJ speedster. (*Photo, Wm. C. Kinsman*)

alloys were selected for the differential housing, oil pan, pistons and connecting rods, firewall, many external engine parts, steering column bracket, torque tube brackets, intake manifold, spare wheel brackets, fuel pump housing, the "timing box" housing, and—finally—even the tail light bracket.

The cost of a Duesenberg chassis ranged from $8500 to $11,750 and included the radiator grille, headlamps, hood, fenders, running boards, and the famous "bow knot" bumpers. From there on it was up to the coachbuilder to satisfy the customer, although, as we shall see, Duesenberg took more than a passing interest in what sort of bodies rode on their chassis. Curiously, what was not furnished for those stiff sums was an appropriate mascot to grace the imperious Duesenberg radiator. The original grilles ventured out onto the streets quite

The Mighty Model "J"

bare, but in 1931 the lightning-like "Duesenbird" became available for $25.00, a curious "extra" in this price range. The "bird" was—at the risk of offending somebody—a rather undistinguished mascot in comparison to Charles Sykes's "Spirit of Ecstasy" on the Rolls-Royce or the *Cigogne Volante* on the Hispano-Suiza, or even the graceful Lincoln greyhound. It seems a curious irony that a good sculptor was not commissioned to create a worthy and typically American mascot for America's best car.

Fred Duesenberg's Model J offered virtually all that could be asked from an automobile: reliability, speed, security, super-status. It was hard to imagine a successor but in 1932 it came; the Model SJ, a flagrant but fascinating gilding of the lily. Basically, the new car was a "J" fitted with a centrifugal type supercharger mounted on the right hand side of the motor which drew the air-gas mixture from the two carburetors and fed it into the pulsing engine at five to eight pounds pressure. The increased demands that the blower made upon the engine and chassis were met with heavier valve springs and larger camshaft bearings, tubular steel connecting rods instead of the J-type alloy rods, and strengthened front suspension.

Two great differences separated the J from the SJ. The first of course was the supercharger and the increased performance which it brought. The concept of the glamorous sounding supercharger went all the way back to Gottlieb Daimler who had toyed with the idea in the 1880s to increase the power output of his small early engines. The technique lay fairly dormant until 1908 when the American Chadwick used a supercharged car to win the "Giants Despair Hill Climb". At about the same time, Marc Birkigt tried two "dead" cylinders functioning as air pumps to create a supercharged version of

Classic elegance at the zenith; a Le Grande touring car on the 142.5-inch chassis. (*Photo, Wm. C. Kinsman*)

the Alphonso XIII Hispano-Suiza, but without notable success. Daimler's company resurrected the supercharger during World War I to help combat oxygen starvation in high flying planes, and immediately after the war applied the idea to a series of small displacement racing cars and later to the famous "S" series supercharged sports cars of the twenties. The principle spread to other makers, even to Bugatti and Bentley who were initially very reluctant about interfering with the purity of their designs.

The refined Duesenberg supercharger, much of which was the work of August Duesenberg, provided a good measure of what the car seemed to need the least of—more ˙speed and acceleration. Unlike the Mercedes-Benz "demand" type supercharger which cut in when the accelerator was floored, the Duesenberg blower was in constant engagement and spun at the rather fearsome velocity of six times the engine speed. The unit now brought the peak engine output to 320 horsepower and the catalogue claimed that "a phaeton with top lowered has been driven 129 MPH in top gear and 104 MPH in second gear". Acceleration was now 0–100 MPH in seventeen seconds through the gears. If he wanted to, the owner of a stock SJ could pull onto a race track and give serious competition to many all-out sports and racing cars.

The second great difference between a J and an SJ, originally at least, was the four great and graceful chromed external exhausts curling out of the right side of the hood. External exhausts appeared early in the century on the 1908 Grand Prix Mercedes and have been symbolic of great power ever since. Outside pipes have often been associated with supercharged cars (particularly on Mercedes) but the two are not necessarily synonymous. The Duesenberg pipes of course had great status significance, being virtually the only way to visually separate an SJ from a J. Even this difference disappeared when the factory, apparently under pressure from

The Mighty Model "J"

rank-conscious J owners, decided to offer an external exhaust installation (without supercharger) for a little over $900. It was obviously a popular option, for, in all, 104 Duesenbergs carried the outside pipes, although only about a third of those (36 to be exact) were genuine, original SJs. So, a Duesenberg with outside pipes is not automatically a supercharged car; you just have to look under the hood to be sure.

E. L. Cord's phenomenal luck finally ran out and his Horatio Alger empire crumbled and fell to the wolves in the summer of 1937. The new owners considered automobile manufacturing on the grand scale outside their province, although a small company was set up to continue service and parts sales to Auburn, Cord, and Duesenberg owners. It was this little company which had the sad task to deliver the last of the line in 1938, an exotic SJ for a rich German who favored the American machine over the European exotica in his garages. Behind this final Duesenberg stretched a line of 470 to 480 (no one is quite sure of the final figure) epic automobiles, and the American continent has not seen the like of them since.

The SJ Duesenberg was the *ne plus ultra* of an already esoteric breed. There was no car in America, and very few in Europe, which could hold a Duesenberg with a determined driver—and none of the few that could came close to three tons of stylish splendour. One of the rare cars on which you might get even money was the 135 MPH Type 57SC Bugatti, an all-out sports/racer with less than half the chassis weight of a J and aircraft type stressed alloy paneling for lightness. Among larger luxury cars there was even less competition. The pseudo-prestigious V–16 Cadillac, supposedly built at a loss by General Motors as a showpiece, offered a very soggy 85–90 MPH while its proliferation of cylinders delivered 4–5 miles to the gallon. The 10,000 pound supercharged 770K Mercedes-Benz could provide fine road security and speeds comfortably over 100 MPH, but it required quite a bit of straight stretch

The Duesenberg

to do it. Rolls-Royce's rare concession to performance, the celebrated and super-elegant Phantom II Continental required more time to reach 60 MPH than the Duesenberg did to reach 100 MPH. One car which could combine spirited performance with Duesenberg-like size, weight, and cachet was Marc Birkigt's 11.3-litre, Type 68-bis Hispano-Suiza.

But perhaps the closest European approach to the Duesenberg was the most ambitious automobile ever attempted, Ettore Bugatti's immortal *Royale*. The two cars were quite different, yet curiously had much in common. Both came from talented individualists whose first love—racing—was clearly carried over into their touring cars. Both, from separate viewpoints, represented the ultimate expression of the straight-eight engine; Duesenberg with double cams and supercharger, and Bugatti with single overhead camshaft and 12.7 litres (14.7 in the prototype car) to produce 300 horsepower at a bare 1700 RPM. Fred Duesenberg's masterpiece could stand comparison in any arena. Traditionally, America lagged behind Europe in the automotive arts, preferring production and promotion to innovation. Duesenberg successfully attacked that tradition as it had never been assaulted before—or since.

5

The Duesenberg Look

In his book, *Classic Cars 1930–1940*, the eminent British motoring writer David Scott-Moncrieff observes that "Duesenberg chassis shared with Rolls-Royce, Hispano-Suiza, Isotta-Fraschini, and a few others the distinction of carrying some of the most flawlessly beautiful coachwork in the world." * For an English critic—and a staunch devotee of Rolls-Royce and Mercedes-Benz automobiles at that—to rise to such heights of rhetoric is indeed rare praise, English understatement notwithstanding. Not that the Duesenberg is not worthy of every word of it, for some examples of Duesenberg bodies represent the very zenith of that grand style of automotive architecture which we call *classic* and the British call *thoroughbred*.

That such great cars were created at all is owed to a unique coincidence—a point in time when craftsmanship and technology were in nearly equal balance. Today, of course, that balance has radically shifted in favor of technology, and most of today's cars rather well show the loss. Recently, in reporting on a new sports car, Denis Jenkinson pointed out that all big

* Used with permission: Robert Bentley, Inc., Publishers, Cambridge, Mass. (*Classic Cars 1930–1940*, out of print).

The Rollston JN sedan of 1935 offered a design of superb balance and style. The car seems to give a pleasing combination of English formality and American dash. (*Photo, Wm. C. Kinsman*)

automakers now have research and development departments. But, in his opinion, the end product of some "hardly seems to justify the means". He could have substituted the word "design department" and the meaning would have been the same. Today, the number of personnel manning the design department at one of the "big three" probably exceeds the number of people involved in most of the custom coachbuilding industry of the Duesenberg era. And it would be interesting to know how

The Rollston JN from a frontal perspective. This car was owned by dancer Bill Robinson. (*Photo, Wm. C. Kinsman*)

Murphy convertible coupe with the rare one-piece exhaust manifold. (*Photo, Wm. C. Kinsman*)

many tons of drafting paper, aspirins, clay models, and command decisions it takes to yield one of today's "look alike" cars.

How then could an archaic industry bereft of computers, plastic, and market analysts come up with so many enduring designs executed with such honest excellence? Part of the answer lay in the flourishing system of custom coachbuilding under which a gentleman was free to buy his automobiles much the same way he bought his suits—custom tailored to his tastes by a craftsman who remained responsive to his client's whims. A customer did not buy a Duesenberg "off the plain pipe rack". (Well, hardly ever!) He was, perhaps, originally

A curious anomaly; a Locke-built town car landaulette in an archly conservative mien mounted on a 100 MPH plus J chassis. (*Photo, Wm. C. Kinsman*)

Pristine Walker roadster; designed by J. Herbert Newport. (*Photo, Wm. C. Kinsman*)

attracted to the marque's merits by one of the now legendary full pages in *Vanity Fair* or like publication which depicted a gentleman at leisure in a baronial study or at the helm of his racing yacht, with the caption "He drives a Duesenberg." It was sublimely subtle or blatantly status-seeking, depending on whether you read Vance Packard, but it ranked with Rolls-Royce's "Best Car in the World" ads. More important, it worked. Despite its esoteric appeal and stratospheric price Duesenberg never lacked for clients and more were out-shopped than of any comparable "super car".

Le style Francais; exotic speedster executed by Fernandez. (*Photo, Wm. C. Kinsman*)

Interior detail of Gary Cooper's Derham Tourster. (*Photo, Wm. C. Kinsman*)

Duesenbergs fitted quite naturally into the ecology of Hollywood of the 1930s; both were larger than life and reveled in the stratospheric. Here, Gary Cooper's celebrated Derham built "Tourster" on the long-wheelbase chassis. (*Photo, Wm. C. Kinsman*)

A trim and sporty touring phaeton executed by Murphy of Pasadena. (*Photo, Wm. C. Kinsman*)

Power and prestige in repose. Le Grande phaeton. (*Photo, J. Herbert Newport*)

Hedonistic; without apology or guilt. The interior of the "Beverly". (*Photo, Wm. C. Kinsman*)

The chic "Beverly" designed by Gordon Buehrig and built by Murphy of Pasadena. (*Photo, Wm. C. Kinsman*)

Duplicate instrument panel and cabinetry in the rear compartment of the "Beverly" sedan by Murphy of Pasadena. (*Photo, Wm. C. Kinsman*)

Once a customer made up his mind that he wanted a Duesenberg between him and the road he was faced with the decision(s) of just what kind of Duesenberg—a racy roadster, a jaunty dual cowl phaeton, a multi-purpose convertible (or "all weather") sedan, or a stately town car? By the early 1930s, the Duesenberg catalogue displayed eighteen models by seven different coachbuilders and these were just suggestions, hors d'oeuvres to whet the customer's appetite. And in the Duesenberg buying stratum of society it was not unlikely that a man might want to refit his entire stable with three or four vehicles,

Massive door and interior detail of a Rollston convertible sedan. (*Photo, Wm. C. Kinsman*)

De gustibus non disputandum est. A draped design interior for a Derham sedan. (*Photo, Wm. C. Kinsman*)

Walter Murphy of Pasadena did this brougham sedan which presents a rather different Duesenberg image. (*Photo, Wm. C. Kinsman*)

Carefully done renderings like this were submitted to prospective Duesenberg customers. Some clients were very certain about what they wanted, others had only vague ideas and sometimes tested the patience of Duesenberg philosophy that the "customer is king". Design by J. Herbert Newport. (*Photo, J. Herbert Newport*)

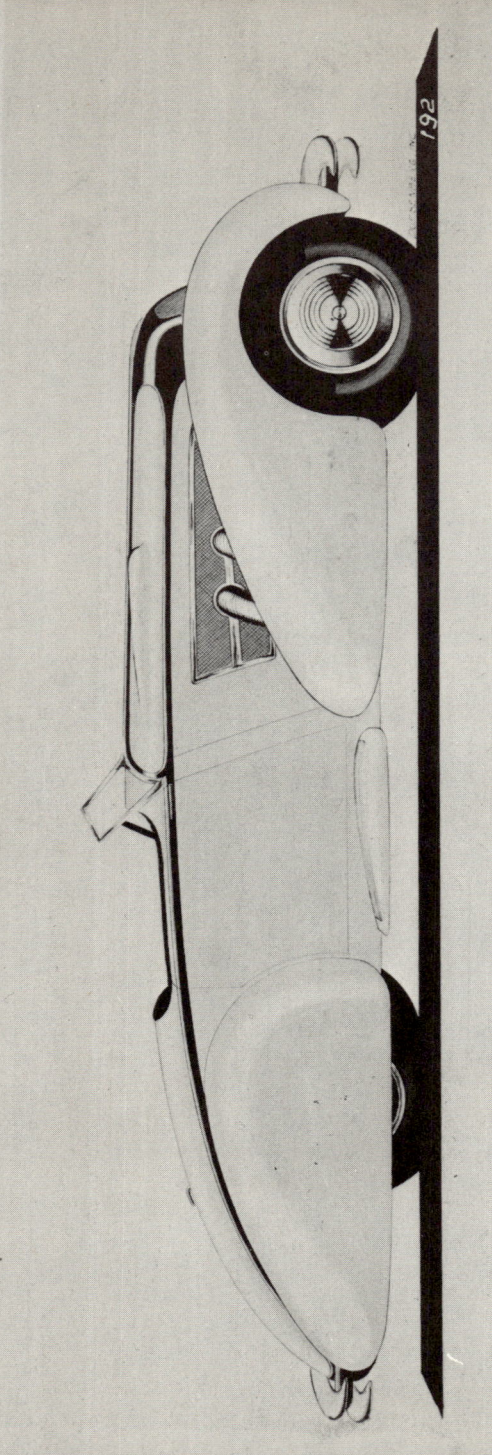

Final designs were sometimes reached only after much trial and error (i.e. customer disapproval). In the process of creating the final SSJ roadster for Gary Cooper this more modernistic approach was tried and rejected in favor of the more classic design. (*Photo, J. Herbert Newport*)

Equipped for any emergency. Lucius Beebe was moved to phrases like "art glass decanters in retractable cabinets . . . Upmann Specials in the humidors, and London Docks cognac imported by 21 brands at $60 a bottle in the folding bars." He thought of it all as the way to "move stylishly". *(Photo, Wm. C. Kinsman)*

A fine piece of cabinetry to grace the owner's compartment of a Brunn limousine. Several decades in time and a whole philosophy apart from the era of plastic "wood" dash panels and vinyl upholstry. *(Photo, Wm. C. Kinsman)*

View of Brunn limousine interior stressing simplicity and quiet elegance. (*Photo, Wm. C. Kinsman*)

A "topless" Duesenberg created for an Arizona sheriff to chase speeders on lawless desert roads. It is unlikely than many escaped. (*Photo, Wm. C. Kinsman*)

The Duesenberg

from a Willoughby town carriage for awesome arrivals at the theatre to a "little" Murphy convertible roadster for his wife to take shopping.

Buyers came in as many assorted shapes and flavors as the cars themselves. Some had only the vaguest notions of what they wanted and leafed lazily through catalogues and sketches while the salesmen kept their patience. Others, like the gentleman who ordered the magnificent and memorable Torpedo Phaeton, knew precisely what they wanted down to the pebble grain finish on the red leather upholstery. That buyer, in fact, toured the factory and personally congratulated each artisan on his particular part in creating the masterpiece. People had a way of becoming very personally involved with the creation of their Duesenbergs; millionaires were known to wander through the plant in coveralls and to listen obediently to mechanics' lectures.

In a custom business where cars were virtually one-of-a-kind (and sometimes literally so), the client was king and his whims were commands. Often it was just these whimsical touches and Duesenberg's devoted attention to them that closed the deal. Over the years Duesenbergs rolled out with rear seat instrument panels, fine cabinetry bars fitted with Baccarat crystal, a built-in jewelry safe, custom fitted Elizabeth Arden vanity case, special compartments for traveling pets, a built-in movie camera, and perhaps the most curious of all—a car fitted with toilet and electric stove!

Normally, the procedure was for the salesman to work out the basics with his customer as to general body style, color, interior decor, and any special little foibles. These were then

Prince Nicholas of Rumania was a royal patron of the Duesenberg art. In addition to his specially built Duesenberg racing car, the Prince owned this Letourneur & Marchand Faux Cabriolet, posed here at the Paris Salon in October, 1931. (*Photo, Wm. C. Kinsman*)

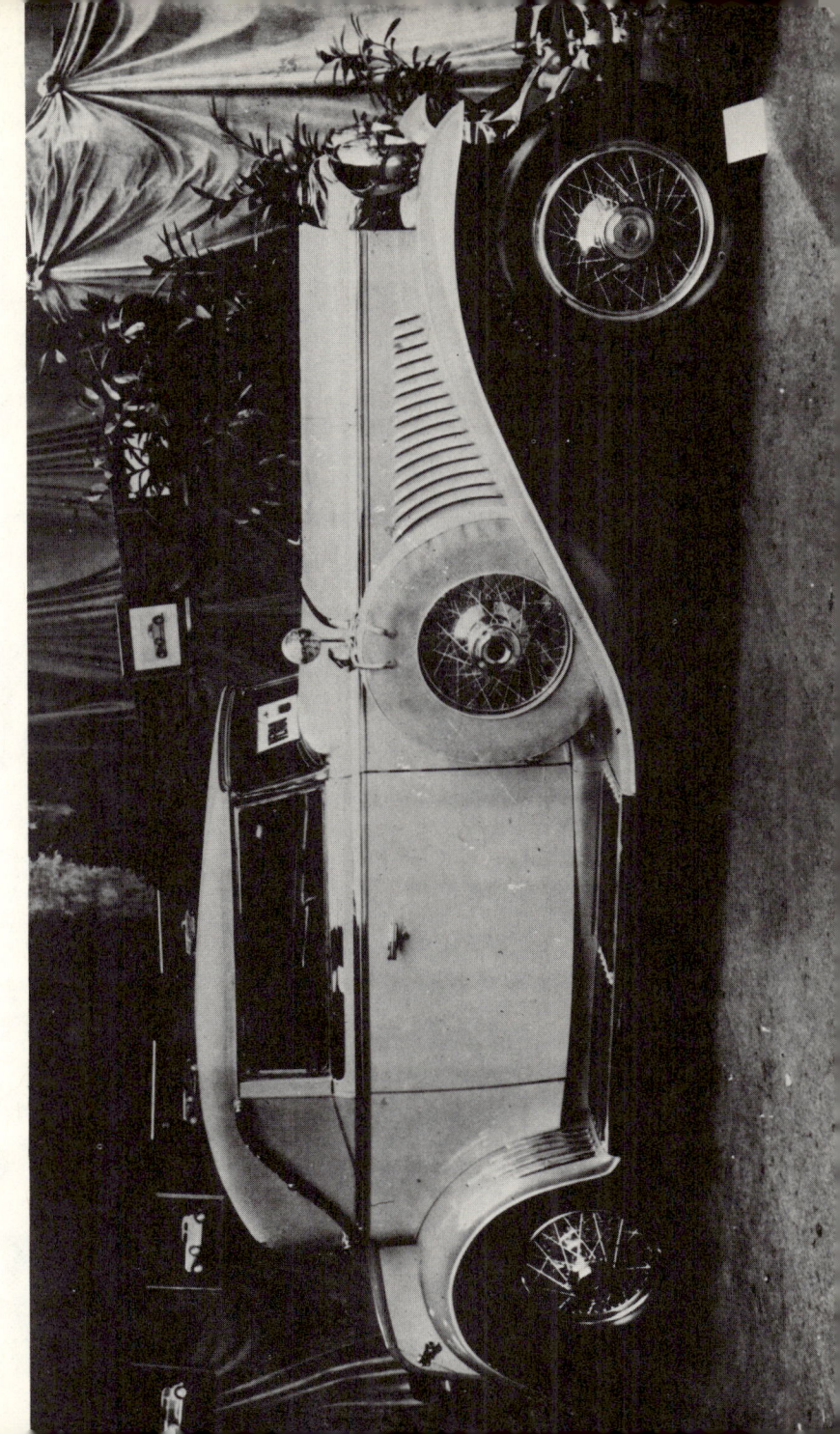

The Duesenberg Look

forwarded to Indianapolis to the Duesenberg body engineer, a capacity virtually created by Duesenberg's Philip A. Derham. Body engineering, rather than just body designing alone, was a Duesenberg strong point, and ensured that a particular body was correct for the chassis. This, among other factors, helped account for the durability and longevity of Duesenbergs. Derham took the salesman's file and from this drew up a set of technical specifications which he sent to the design department. Working with this technical information and the customer's aesthetics, the designer then produced one or more pencil outline sketches which were discussed with the engineer. They decided which one best integrated engineering and art and then the body designer did a color rendering which was sent out to the customer. This step might produce a reaction somewhere between ecstasy and horror and alterations were made accordingly. An interesting variation on the process was used for awhile by the coachbuilding firm of Walter M. Murphy of Pasadena, California, which built more Duesenbergs than any other single coachbuilder. Murphy designers would draw the proposed car full scale on a giant blackboard so that the actual dimensions could be appreciated.

Throughout this crucial stage, the attitude that the customer was right was maintained, and eventually came that moment of truth when the buyer accepted the final design and said, "Go ahead and build it." Then, a small scale layout of the body was made up and submitted for bids to selected coachbuilders for cost and delivery date estimates. Selection of a suitable coachbuilder was a significant decision. Despite the prestige of building a body on the finest chassis in the country, most of the coachbuilders found Duesenberg a minor account because

Aristocrat. A "Faux (false) Cabriolet" by Letourneur & Marchand built for the Marquis de Portago. American Duesenbergs were quite revered in Europe. (*Photo, Wm. C. Kinsman*)

Class at the curbside—a magnificent Murphy convertible roadster on a J chassis. (*Photo, Wm. C. Kinsman*)

of the relatively small volume of business, and at a given time they might be committed to a run of bread and butter cars. Most, however, were delighted to get their coachbuilder's plate on a Duesenberg chassis and gave the company service well out of proportion to the size of their account.

Choosing the right coachbuilder was a delicate task which could possibly make or break the completed car because some builders were specialists in particular styles and their expertise and experience could be relied upon. If the car being built, for instance, was to have a very reserved and formal flavor, the

The European idiom on a J chassis; a "Transformable Imperial" thought to have been built by Fernandez. (*Photo, Wm. C. Kinsman*)

Lush leather, laid out for comfort. Design by J. Herbert Newport. (*Photo, J. Herbert Newport*)

Willoughby Company was a good choice. If, on the other hand, the customer's tastes tended toward the dashing and even the spectacular, Walter Murphy or Bohman and Schwartz were good choices. And if the customer happened to be a Hollywood star both Murphy and Bohman and Schwartz were conveniently nearby in Pasadena for last minute changes and suggestions. Between these two poles was a firm like Rollston in New York, possibly the most English-influenced of the four-

A quite unconventional phaeton executed by De Franay coachbuilders. (*Photo, Wm. C. Kinsman*)

teen domestic coachbuilders who built for Duesenberg, which could deftly combine both quiet reserve and dramatic flair.

Once the selection of a coachbuilder had been made, the body engineer was often called upon to play something of a master diplomat to co-ordinate the preferences of Duesenberg, the body builder, and the customer. It could be, to say the least, an unenviable responsibility. Along with the small scale layout of the body, the coachbuilder also received the designer's renderings of the interior design, with particular details of any special niceties such as tulipwood cocktail cabinets or airtight cigar humidors.

In a few cases the bodies were fully completed and even mounted on the chassis at the coachbuilder's shop. This would be the case where—in those relatively rare instances—the company sold the bare chassis only and the owner preferred to make his own arrangements with a coachbuilder. Also, this was usually a more workable arrangement where European builders such as Saoutchik, Hibbert & Darrin, Letourneur & Marchand, or Castagne were called upon to create on the Duesenberg chassis. However, in most cases the coachbuilder did the body "in the white", that is, metal work and special fittings only without paint or trim. At this point the semi-completed body was shipped to Indianapolis. There it was mounted on the chassis, lacquered and the final trim installed. All things considered, this seems like an inefficient way to build an automobile, part here and part there, but then it would also have been more *efficient* for Michelangelo to have painted the Sistine Chapel ceiling with a roller.

A design originally done by J. Herbert Newport for a car for the Shah of Persia but never built for him. The design was subsequently altered and later the car appeared as the famous "Father Divine throne car" built by Bohman & Schwartz. (*Photo, J. Herbert Newport*)

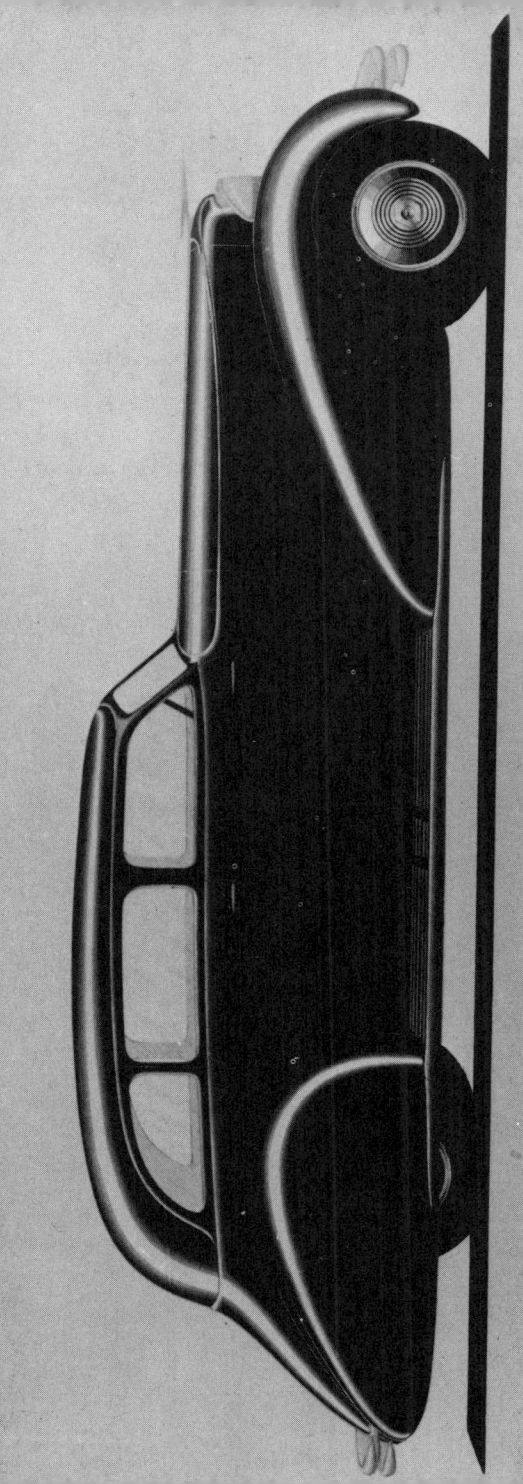

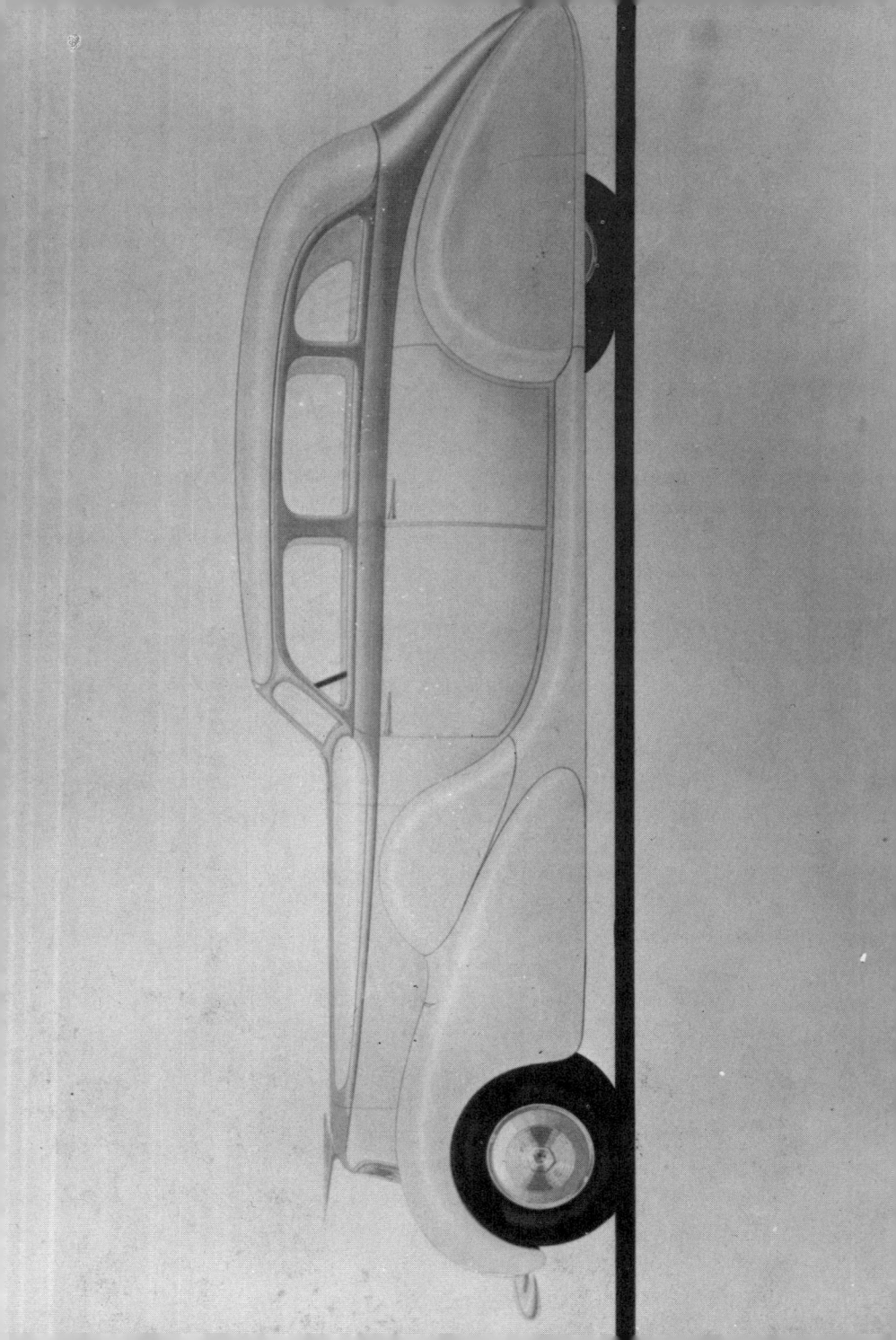

Clay model of a Duesenberg that never was; the $7500 "economy" model which was in the planning stage when the company expired in 1937. (*Photo, J. Herbert Newport*)

This procedure of mounting, painting, and trimming the body on Duesenberg premises also had the advantage of giving the designer almost complete control over his creation. It did not leave the final, and often crucial, interpretation of the design solely to the coachbuilder.

Duesenberg's personal interest in their product is of course legendary; August Duesenberg is said to have personally inspected every car to come out of the plant and every single car was individually tested on the Indianapolis Speedway with

Another prospective design for the Shah of Persia which included rear facing jump seats so that no passenger could turn his back to the potentate. The Shah's son spent several weeks at the factory while designing was going on to study American manufacturing techniques. (*Photo, J. Herbert Newport*)

The Duesenberg

little more than a driver's seat bolted onto the chassis. This strong personal interest also extended to the coachwork; Duesenberg was rather circumspect about what sort of bodies were to be carried on their chassis and maintained perhaps more control over the final appearance of the car than the builders of any other grand marque did with their own. This policy of company control did much toward maintaining that certain indefinable "Duesenberg Look", even in the face of great customer freedom. Many Duesenbergs were extremely individualistic cars, yet despite styling swings from the most staid town cars to exuberant boat-tailed speedsters most were instantly recognizable as Duesenbergs.

Although Duesenberg's main concern was the production of chassis, the company always remained paternalistic about what was to ride on those chassis and was always very active in body design. Their advertising claimed that "Duesenberg maintains a custom designing and body engineering department second to none in the world. They originate more new designs and actually build more individual bodies than any other custom company." Even in those unusual cases where the bare chassis was sold separately and the customer made his own arrangements for coachwork, the "Duesenberg Look" was still maintained by the company's policy of supplying the distinctive radiator grille, hood, headlamps, characteristic "clamshell" fenders, running boards, and the "bow knot" bumpers along with the chassis.

Sometimes the Duesenberg determination to preserve its characteristic charisma was aided by a customer's impatience

The practice of custom coachbuilding permitted radical departures from the regular run of things. Working with his client, Eli Lilly of the Indianapolis drug company, J. Herbert Newport designed this very unusual Duesenberg coupe which was built by Walker-Le Grande. (*Photo, Wm. C. Kinsman*)

Radiator detail of the Walker-Le Grande. The grille was slightly V-shaped which meant that each of the strips had to be hand made to an individual length. Construction of the grille from 5/8 inch and 3/4 inch strips cost $500, plus another $500 for plating. (*Photo, Wm. C. Kinsman*)

If a buyer did not have very specific ideas in mind beyond the selection of a basic body style, such as a sedan or roadster, he might not want to go through the whole custom creation process. Such less demanding customers permitted Duesenberg to pre-order batches or sanctions of popular bodies to be

Profile of the unconventional Walker-Le Grande coupe for Eli Lilly. (*Photo, Wm. C. Kinsman*)

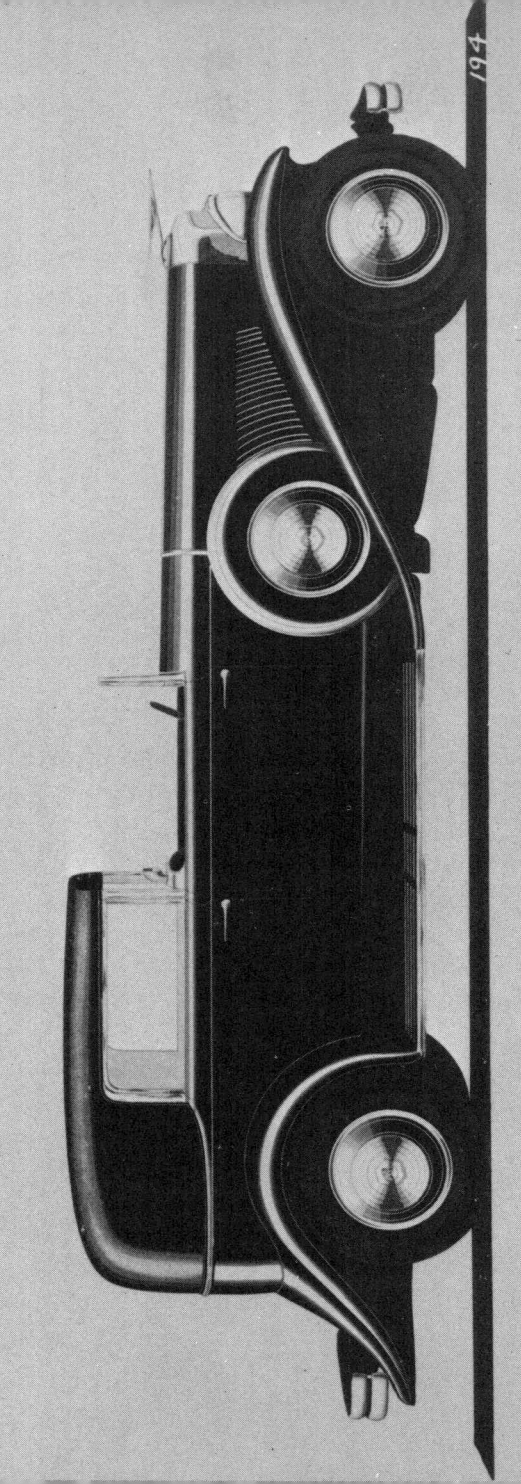

The Duesenberg Look

made up in the white, and then finish, paint, and trim them out in their own shop to the customer's preferences. Such "semi-custom" building was quicker and a little cheaper, but did not result in "look alike" cars because even two identical bodies could be finished and detailed out in so many different ways that they virtually seemed to be two different cars.

At the other end of the spectrum, Duesenberg also turned out some very special cars for special people, and some of them have gone down into legend. There is probably no more famous or more frequently photographed Duesenberg than the exciting SSJ sports roadster built on the specially shortened 125-inch-wheelbase chassis. There were originally only two such fabulous cars, one for Clark Gable—who remained an aficionado of great cars until his death—and one for Gary Cooper, who also drove an enormous and imposing Derham "Tourster" built on the long 153.5-inch-wheelbase chassis. The co-author of this book is pleased and proud to have been the designer of the esoteric pair of SSJ Duesenbergs, and is presently in the process of creating a third SSJ on a shortened SJ chassis for Mr. John C. North II of Easton, Maryland. It is an exciting and challenging project, and one which proves that with taste and imagination, and some patience, great cars in the classic tradition are still possible in the 1970s.

Quite a few Duesenbergs were sold to the 1930's equivalent of the "Beautiful People", and these cars usually matched their owners as choice pieces of exotica extraordinaire. Duesenbergs fitted quite naturally into the ecology of Hollywood in the Thirties; both were larger than life and unabashedly reveled in the stratospheric. Duesenbergs populated the rococo, baroque, or Gothic garages of people like Richard Arlen, Marion Davies (who owned a pair of formals; a convertible town car and a

A Duesenberg town car design drawn by J. Herbert Newport for Mae West in 1934. (*Photo, J. Herbert Newport*)

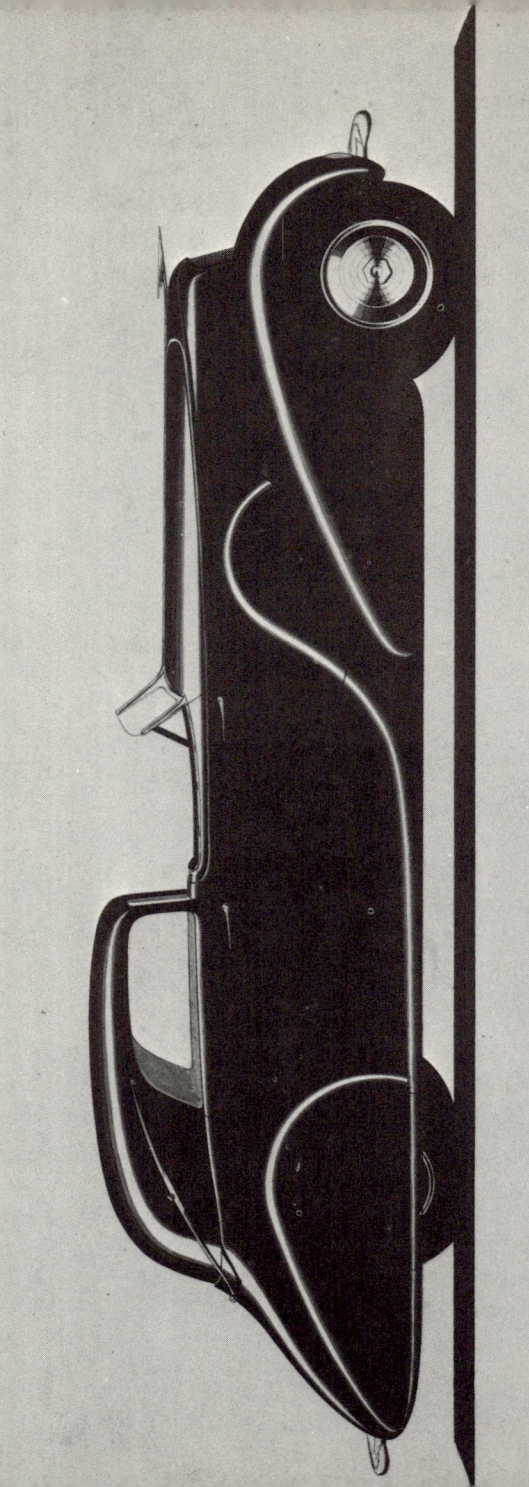

Perspectives of the proposed town car for Mae West, 1934. (*Photo, J. Herbert Newport*)

lush "opera brougham"), Lupe Velez, Mae West (who looked perhaps more at home in the back of a liveried town car than any of the others), Joe E. Brown, Paul Whiteman. Though he is now said to favor a 1959 Chevrolet, in his Hollywood days even a convention-flouting billionaire named Howard Hughes drove a Dusie. A few Duesenbergs also filtered through to mere millionaires (Philip Wrigley owned five of them) and became the hallmark of that thin stratum of society on which

A design originally created by J. Herbert Newport for Mae West in 1934. The car was later built for Mrs. Ethel V. Mars by Bohman & Schwartz. (*Photo, J. Herbert Newport*)

The Duesenberg

Lucius Beebe liked to lavish phrases like "the arbiters of effulgence".

Although even the mighty Duesenberg could not quite wean him from his beloved Rolls-Royces, the car from Indianapolis was a machine to gladden the heart of a man like the late Lucius who loved all things done in the grand manner without apology, and loved above all to "move stylishly" in road vehicle, private railway car, or via Cunard. His description of those select few cars was typical: "A common denominator of all these cars of *Grande Marque* were the severe faced chauffeurs, the jeweled traveling clocks and vanities, the mink lap robes, the art glass decanters in retractable cabinets, and the beautiful West of England cloth upholstery. Many of them represented an investment of $30,000 on the hoof, as it were, with ceilings painted by celebrated muralists, Upmann Specials in the humidors, and London Docks cognac imported by 21 Brands at $60 a bottle in the folding bars."

Again typical, he recalled that "James J. Walker, Mayor of New York in the Thirties, had a $20,000 Duesenberg town car, reportedly the gift of an admirer, A. C. Blumenthal. It had yellow basketwork for its body and the Mayor liked to use it when attending Board of Estimate meetings to discuss civic matters of pith and moment. 'Keep your motor running, I won't be long', he told the chauffeur. After moments among the financial audits he would take a farewell of his colleagues. 'Keep your hands to the plow, dear friends!', he would tell them in leaving."

As we have seen, affluent Americans traditionally turned to Europe for their motorized carriages *de grande luxe*. It took Duesenberg to reverse the trend, to send Europeans shopping

Rollston-built JN convertible coupe represented an updated version of the popular Murphy roadster. J. Herbert Newport design. (*Photo, Wm. C. Kinsman*)

The Duesenberg Look

for an American car. Europeans had known the name Duesenberg to be something special since the celebrated victory in the 1921 French Grand Prix, but it was not until the J and SJ models began to land on the Continent that they really began to take notice, and to write checks in Duesenberg's Parisian showroom.

Kings, Queens, and Heads of State used Duesenbergs, but none with more propaganda value than His Majesty King Alfonso XIII of Spain who bought magnificent automobiles with the fancy that most people buy phonograph records or magazines. The young king first became enthralled with cars when the original Hispano-Suizas were being built in Spain before World War I. The early sports Hisso was named "the Alfonso XIII" and the King became Hispano's best customer and public relations piece. Later, he ordered the first Bugatti *Royale*, although the car was never actually delivered. However, this royal connoisseur's favorite car was his French-bodied Duesenberg which he reportedly selected as the only car from his sprawling collection when the Spanish Monarchy ended rather abruptly in 1931.

Prince Nicolas of Rumania was another avid royal patron of the Duesenberg art. In addition to a lush personal car, the Prince drove a specially built Duesenberg racing car. It was well known on the European circuits in the 1930s, although the Prince never achieved his ultimate ambition with the car—to win at Le Mans.

In terms of gold-backed dollars of the 1930s a Duesenberg represented a very substantial investment. The original bare chassis price of the J was $8500 and later increased to $9500. Cost of clothing the chassis was, of course, whatever the buyer wanted to spend, and often that was considerable. The lowest

Same JN convertible coupe with the top down. (*Photo, Wm. C. Kinsman*)

The last of the line. An exotic SJ delivered in 1938 to a rich German who favored the American machine over the European cars in his garages. (*Photo, Wm. C. Kinsman*)

price ever mentioned for a body was for a basic Murphy roadster at $2500, although it is open to question whether any were actually built this inexpensively. From records compiled by the Automobile Manufacturers Association in Detroit, it would appear, in fact, that even as early as 1929 the very cheapest

A car for the man who asked Fred Duesenberg to build "the finest thing on four wheels." E. L. Cord's personal Duesenberg limousine by Brunn, interior design by J. Herbert Newport. (*Photo, Wm. C. Kinsman*)

Vertical and vital; front-on view of E. L. Cord's Brunn-built Duesenberg limousine. (*Photo, J. Herbert Newport*)

body cost $3500, thus making the most economical Duesenberg about $12,000. Other prices quoted that year rose to $25,000, including "two fender wells and six wire wheels standard." Shortly even these basics went up. The Association's 1932 listing describes a "Murphy convertible coupe" for $13,500, a "Rollston convertible Victoria" for $14,750 and a "Derham Phaeton" for the same price. Everything, of course, jumped again when the supercharged SJ came out in 1932 with a bare chassis price of $11,750.

Convertible sedan by Walter M. Murphy Company of Pasadena, California. (*Photo, Wm. C. Kinsman*)

The Duesenberg

Some quite fantastic sums have been bandied about for Duesenbergs, although it is fairly well established that the majority of the domestically built cars cost under $20,000. This is not to say that the price was an "un-fantastic" sum to pay for an automobile in the 1930s when a quite nice house could be bought for about the same price. However, gilded lilies always attract attention and a select few "super cars" served as impressive public relations pieces. The famous "Twenty Grand" by Rollston and the original Torpedo Phaeton (which cost even a little more) were good examples of such publicized showpieces. Then, behind the exotic comes the outlandish. Ken Purdy tells of a maharaja who glorified the rear compartment with magnificent Nain Persian carpeting which he claimed cost "several times" as much as the car.

Prices on the European built Duesenbergs tended to run higher, both for the basic cost and for shipping, customs duties, and purchase taxes. Some strikingly handsome bodies were produced by European artist/craftsmen and these characteristically Continental designs gave the Duesenberg a genuinely international cachet.

The golden age of custom coachbuilding which produced the Duesenberg in all its glory is, lamentably, no longer with us. Although modern techniques applied to an old art, new materials, and most of all a renewed interest in cars with character promise at least a mini-revival. Generally, except for a few diplomatic and royal cars, the wheeled foibles of oil-rich shieks and special jobs for eccentrics like Nubar Gulbenkian, gone are the days when a man who could afford a prestige car could also have it tailored to his own tastes by a bespoke coachbuilder who was as sensitive to individual preference as a Saville Row cloth cutter. That golden era produced some superb blendings of chassis and the coachbuilder's art, but none was more magnificently many splendored than "the finest thing on four wheels".

6

Duesenberg at Speed

Duesenberg has traditionally been a name synonymous with speed and exhilarating performance on both road and track. In the years that the J and SJ Duesenbergs were offered for sale they were the fastest standard production cars that you could buy across any counter in the world. Duesenberg's quite intentional image as a willing and extraordinarily fast car added much to its esoteric aura. Whether psychologists choose to explain it as ego satisfaction, masculinity assurance for aging millionaires, or simple status-seeking, those mental pictures of a throbbing, unpassable Duesenberg rushing into the sunset certainly helped to sell cars.

The Duesenberg penchant for fast machines dated back to the very beginning of the Duesenberg dynasty. Even the original little two cylinder Mason was conceived to be faster than the ordinary run of cars, and if nothing else it served to hook Fred Duesenberg on the idea that fast, successful racing cars were the best advertising that a motorcar builder could buy. Like the fire breathers of modern Detroit, the little Mason laid a heavy hand on undisguised speed to sell the product.

Duesenberg at Speed

Speed was the stock-in-trade of the shoestring Duesenberg racing organization in the pioneer days before World War I. At the demise of the Mason-Maytag venture, Duesenberg had acquired the right to use the established "Mason" name, but the cars that carried it now were new and purely Duesenberg. Everyone from Fred and Augie and their young racing driver named Eddie Rickenbacker to the mechanics had plenty of faith and enthusiasm in the team, although they had little else. Today, in his autobiography, Eddie Rickenbacker looks back to that far-away world of milk shake lunches and sixteen-hour work days building and racing Fred Duesenberg's cars. He recalls that in 1913 the team's assets had shrunk to three Masons and spare parts, seven silver dollars, and a mascot cat named Lady Luck.

It was an exciting but bleak existence and the only hope of salvation lay in the big three-hundred-mile race at Sioux City, Iowa, which in those days ranked with Indianapolis in prestige and prize money. Despite their reduced circumstances, the Duesenberg team had the experience, skill, and determination needed to win a big time race. All they really needed was luck and Rickenbacker undertook to supply that. Recalling one of his mother's Swiss folkways, on the day of the race Rickenbacker tied a bat's heart to his middle finger with a red silk thread—a guaranteed talisman of good fortune!

The future "Captain Eddie" needed his bat's heart, a rabbit's foot, four-leaf clover, and whatever else he could get for the murderous three hundred miles which lay before him. First, there was a popular driver named Spencer Wishart driving a

Eddie Rickenbacker at the wheel of one of Fred Duesenberg's "Mason" racers posing at Indianapolis in 1914. These were the days when the team fortunes oscillated between a few silver dollars and milkshake lunches to glory and grand prizes. (*Photo, Indianapolis Motor Speedway*)

powerful Mercer which outgunned the Mason. Then, as the race wore on, the very track itself became a deadly enemy as great chunks of the paving surface were kicked up by the cars and pelted other cars and drivers like deadly hailstones. Rickenbacker had quickly concocted a screen of wire mesh to shield himself and his riding mechanic. However, as he pressed Wishart in the Mercer, the hail of paving surface became so fierce that it knocked down his wire "cage" and Rickenbacker and his mechanic were exposed to the machine gun-like hail. A few minutes later a big chunk of the "gumbo" paving hit Rickenbacker's riding mechanic and knocked him unconscious, leaving Eddie to drive, work the manual oil pump, and to try to keep a check on tire wear. Suddenly, another car veered in front of Rickenbacker's Mason in an attempt to avoid a third car. Rickenbacker pulled the wheel just in time to avoid a full collision, but his front wheels nicked the rear of the other car and it went careening through a fence and crashed to a halt with all four wheels in the air. Rickenbacker had only a glimpse of the accident and did not know until later that both the driver and his riding mechanic had been killed.

The Mason continued the deadly duel with the Mercer and in the end Rickenbacker beat the favorite Wishart home by over half a minute. And behind the Mercer came another Mason driven by Tom Alley to raise the Duesenberg prize money to $12,500. There may be something to bat's hearts and red silk thread after all, but not nearly as much as there is to a skilled and determined driver in a fine car.

The first postwar Duesenberg, and by then appearing under its rightful name, was of course the "Straight Eight" which received as much tempering on the track as it did on test benches. The Eight was a three-litre or 183 cubic inches of single overhead-camshaft design and its racing edition appeared on a one-hundred-inch-wheelbase chassis. The first cars were ready before the end of 1919, which had not been a bad

Fred Duesenberg's long awaited dream, a victory at Indianapolis, finally came in 1924, and in the next year Duesenberg repeated the feat with Peter DePaolo in "Number 12", which was the first Indy car in history to average over 100 MPH. (*Photo, Indianapolis Motor Speedway*)

racing season for Duesenberg even with the old four-cylinder cars. The new Duesenberg racers were a success at speed right from the beginning; the initial tests were at Sheepshead Bay Speedway on Long Island and the new records which the Straight Eight set there were just hints of what was to come. In 1920, Duesenberg victories blossomed across America from Uniontown, Pennsylvania, to Beverly Hills, California. Although still not yet a winner at Indianapolis (Duesenberg was third, fourth, and sixth that year), the brothers could temporarily be comforted by the spectacular 1–2–3–4 finish at the Uniontown race.

If a Duesenberg straight-eight engine was fast, then two of them bolted into a single chassis had to be out of sight. This was precisely what Duesenberg proposed to do to create a record car which would permanently link "Duesenberg" and "speed" in the public mind. The inspiration for the "double eight Duesenberg" may have come from the war-built Bugatti sixteen-cylinder engine which also used the idea of twin eights mounted side by side. However, inspiration was a long way from reality and putting together a workable record car with twin engines and separate drive shafts to the rear axle and devising a suitable aerodynamic wedge body—all on a limited expense account—called for a lot of doing. The brothers did it, however, and their car also did it—a new record for the mile of 156.04 MPH set on April 27, 1920, at Daytona Beach with Tommy Milton at the wheel.

The following year, another Duesenberg at speed was destined to do what no American car had ever done before and what would take nearly half a century for another American car to equal. Appropriately, it fell to Duesenberg to be the first American car ever to win a European *grande épreuve* race. Anyone who has ever had more than a scant paragraph to say about Duesenberg has remarked that Jimmy Murphy vanquished Europe's best Grand Prix machinery to win the 1921 French Grand Prix in a three-litre Duesenberg. Most commentators have had little more to say about that signal event in motoring history than to record the bare statistic, a slight which shall be remedied forthwith.

Duesenberg could hardly have chosen a better showcase for the new straight-eight than the Auto Club de France's Grand Prix of 1921. The first Grand Prix since 1914, the race was sure to attract intense European (and worldwide) attention, and for an American car to give a good account of itself would in-

The starting line-up for the 1921 French Grand Prix, the last time the cars were started in pairs. The Duesenbergs are (L to R) #6 with Guyot standing in front of the left rear wheel, #12 Jimmy Murphy's car, #16 Joe Boyer's car, and #13 (extreme right) driven by Dubonnet. (*Photo, Jerry Gebby*)

deed be a coup. However, the race was also sure to attract a very determined French contingent which still remembered the debacle at Lyons in the last Grand Prix in 1914 when the "invincible" Henry-engined Peugeots were devastated by the famous Mercedes 1–2–3 victory.

The German victory at Lyons had been the result of fine machinery run with precise planning and management. It was a lesson which Duesenberg certainly did not overlook in selecting George Robertson as team manager. Robertson's racing experience dated back to pioneer days; his greatest moment of glory was winning the 1908 Vanderbilt Cup race on Long

The 1921 French Grand Prix soon evolved into a hot contest between the American Duesenbergs and French Ballots. Here, Ballot number one with Ralph De Palma at the wheel is about to be overtaken by Jimmy Murphy in Duesenberg number 12. Murphy's riding mechanic Olson is trying to wave the Ballot over to gain passing room, but both De Palma and DePaolo seem oblivious. (*Photo, Jerry Gebby*)

Island before 200,000 spectators on perhaps the most famous American racing machine of all, "Old Sixteen", a monster Locomobile of sixteen-litres displacement. Robertson apparently took his team manager's duties quite seriously for the Duesenberg team arrived in France—although late—considerably better prepared than their French rivals, who had again fallen into their characteristic over-confidence. Some of the French drivers even considered practice runs as superfluous nuisances.

Duesenberg at Speed

Duesenberg entered four cars (at an enormous late entry fee of 86,500 francs) and sportingly split the team down the middle between French and American drivers. The Americans were Jimmy Murphy and Joe Boyer; the Frenchmen Albert Guyot and Andre Dubonnet. All were professionals except Dubonnet who was a talented amateur driver who preferred fast cars to administering the family liqueur fortune. He was always the flamboyant "gentleman driver" in the grand manner, and in this race appeared at the starting line with bright blue silk helmet and face scarf.

The Duesenberg Grand Prix cars which appeared on the Sarthe Circuit at Le Mans represented the cream of American machinery. With three-litre displacement, they complied to both Indianapolis and Auto Club de France regulations of the

Victory for America. Number 12 takes the flag to become the first U.S. car to win a European Grand Prix. In the last French G.P. before World War I the French lost their Grand Prix to the Germans and in this first post-war revival they lost to the Americans, so the stands were stoically silent as the flag fell. (*Photo, Jerry Gebby*)

The Duesenberg

day. The A.C.F. also stipulated a minimum weight of 800 kilos (1763 pounds) which the Duesenberg more than met at 910–926 kilos. The engines were of single overhead-camshaft layout with three valves per cylinder, two exhaust and one inlet. Interestingly, the cylinders were not bored vertically but were slightly inclined. Fitted with four Miller carburetors, the engine gave off 115–120 horsepower at 4250 RPM.

The much-mentioned hydraulic braking system which used glycerine and water as fluid was the first such system ever to appear on a racing car and was the talk of aficionados at Le Mans. To everyone's surprise, the Duesenberg brakes performed flawlessly, causing an English commentator on the scene to observe that "the Duesenberg hydraulic method of

The stress of a harrowing race (Joe Boyer called it "a damn rock hewing contest.") is clearly visible on Olson's face as he holds the trophy of the 1921 French Grand Prix while Murphy manages a smile. (*Photo, Jerry Gebby*)

One of the historic racing cars of American motorsport; Duesenberg number 12 in which Jimmy Murphy won America's first victory in a European Grand Prix race at Le Mans in 1921. Car is permanently on display at the Indianapolis Motor Speedway Museum parked in front of scenes from its moment of glory in France. (*Photo, Indianapolis Motor Speedway*)

operation appeared to stand the strain better than any other (braking system)".

The Duesenbergs were well matched at Le Mans, for Europe, too, had almost universally turned to the straight-eight as a "standard" racing machine, most marques preferring the double overhead-cam approach which of course remained in vogue on the circuits into the 1950s. Duesenberg's chief rival on the Sarthe was the Ballot team of four cars which, with one exception, relied on a new double overhead-cam four-valves-per-cylinder car which most everyone touted as the favorite of the day. The exception was a two-litre, four-cylinder Ballot which did so well (finally finishing third) that it threatened the creditability of the multi-cylinder machines. Duesenberg's other competition consisted primarily of the Anglo-French Sunbeam-Talbot-Darracq combine, a much magnified threat which diminished as the race progressed.

The Duesenberg

On Monday, July 25th, 1921, under an overcast sky the cars were sent off in pairs, the last time that the old style start was used. The course was rather short at seventeen kilometers or 10¾ miles, which ensured that something of interest was generally happening in front of the stands. The first lap was an accurate preview of what was coming; a hot contest between Duesenberg and Ballot with Joe Boyer on Duesenberg and Ralph De Palma on Ballot each setting up identical lap times of eight minutes and sixteen seconds. Murphy's Duesenberg

Historic pause. Ralph De Palma and his riding mechanic and protégé Peter DePaolo. De Palma and DePaolo opposed Duesenberg in the 1921 French Grand Prix and finished second behind Murphy and Olson. (*Photo, Smith Hempstone Oliver*)

DUESENBERG STRAIGHT EIGHT

Winning the Grand Prix, France, July, 1921
The First and Only American Car to Win a European Classic

In body design and in all the details that go to insure the last word in convenient motoring elegance and comfort the Duesenberg is as much a leader as it is in scientific engineering. The glimpse of the last type bodies on pages eight and nine convey but an idea of the types of standard bodies that are mounted on the standard Duesenberg chassis at the factory. A very large number of Duesenberg chassis are sent to custom builders for mounting of special bodies selected by patrons. Even the standard open and closed body types shown in this booklet are produced for Duesenberg by the master coach-builders of the country. The coach upholstery, finish and every detail of equipment is in thorough accord with the superb chassis with its pre-eminent engineering features.

DUESENBERG AUTOMOBILE AND MOTORS COMPANY, INC.

Duesenberg capitalized on the 1921 French Grand Prix victory in its advertising. Here a page from the Duesenberg catalogue proclaims Duesenberg as "The first and only American car to win a European classic", a claim which remained valid until the Ford victories at Le Mans in the 1960s. *(Photo, Jerry Gebby)*

was third at eight minutes and twenty one seconds, again the precise time as Jules Chassagne's fourth place Ballot. The interesting coincidence of identical lap times persisted into the second lap when Jimmy Murphy and Joe Boyer moved into

Fred Duesenberg, builder of the winning car, congratulates its driver, Peter de Paolo, after he took the checkered flag at Indianapolis, breaking all records for this world famous event with an average speed of 101.13 miles per hour.

It had long been the Duesenberg dream to win the Indianapolis 500. The dream was realized in 1924, and here there was a repeat performance in 1925 when Peter DePaolo brought home his Duesenberg in first place at an average speed of 101.13 MPH to break all records for the "500". Fred Duesenberg congratulates Peter DePaolo just after the victory. (*Photo, Smith Hempstone Oliver*)

first and second places after sixteen minutes and thirteen seconds of total elapsed time.

Driving this Grand Prix called for an endurance which harked back to the early days of racing, for the course was badly prepared for these fast, high-performing machines. In a short time the track was cut up into loose gravel and the hail of flying stones which sprayed out like buckshot from behind each car quickly accounted for a large share of casualties, both

The "Mormon Meteor" body design and construction must have set some sort of record for efficiency; the first full layout of drawings was ready a week after Jenkin's arrival at the factory and were approved by him except for the location of the driver's step plate. The car was then built without a single deviation from the plans. (*Photo, J. Herbert Newport*)

Ab Jenkins ... auto driver, either holds or shares 145 of the 232 records in the A.A.A. contest board books as of Oct. 1, 1936. 113 are unlisted ...

mechanical and human. The riding mechanic in Albert Guyot's Duesenberg was knocked unconscious and had to be replaced, while in one of the Talbots Colonel Seagrave's companion suffered the same fate and was carried five miles before he came to. The cars suffered even more; Chassagne's fuel tank was knocked loose by flying stones and fell onto the drive shaft, which immediately put him out of the running. The Darracq driven by Rene Thomas had its oil tank riddled (as was Seagrave's) and virtually every car in the race was running with a leaky radiator punctured by flying stones. In fact, the wining Duesenberg ran the last two laps just about bone dry, a grand tribute to the stamina of the engine. Joe Boyer, whose Duesenberg went out in the eighteenth lap with a snapped connecting rod, characterized the race as "a damn rock hewing contest."

By the tenth lap Duesenberg held first, third, and fourth places and the French spectators realized that it was going to be a fight to the bitter end. No flash in the pan, these Yankees. Two laps later French hopes soared as Murphy, the leader, pulled in for a pit stop and Chassagne's Ballot took the lead. The enthusiasm was short-lived for it was in the seventeenth lap when Chassagne lost his fuel tank and Murphy moved back in the lead, with Albert Guyot's Duesenberg supporting him in number two spot. From the twentieth to the twenty-fifth lap the lead positions remained stable, although Andre Dubonnet moved his Duesenberg into fourth, just behind Ralph De Palma's Ballot. After this, Guyot's Duesenberg be-

---

The J and SJ were not competitively exploited as the Model A had been, but in 1935 the company decided to field a record car. August Duesenberg reworked a standard 142.5-inch-wheelbase SJ chassis to give 400 HP and J. Herbert Newport designed a special one-of-a-kind body for the record car to be driven by "Ab" Jenkins. (*Photo, J. Herbert Newport*)

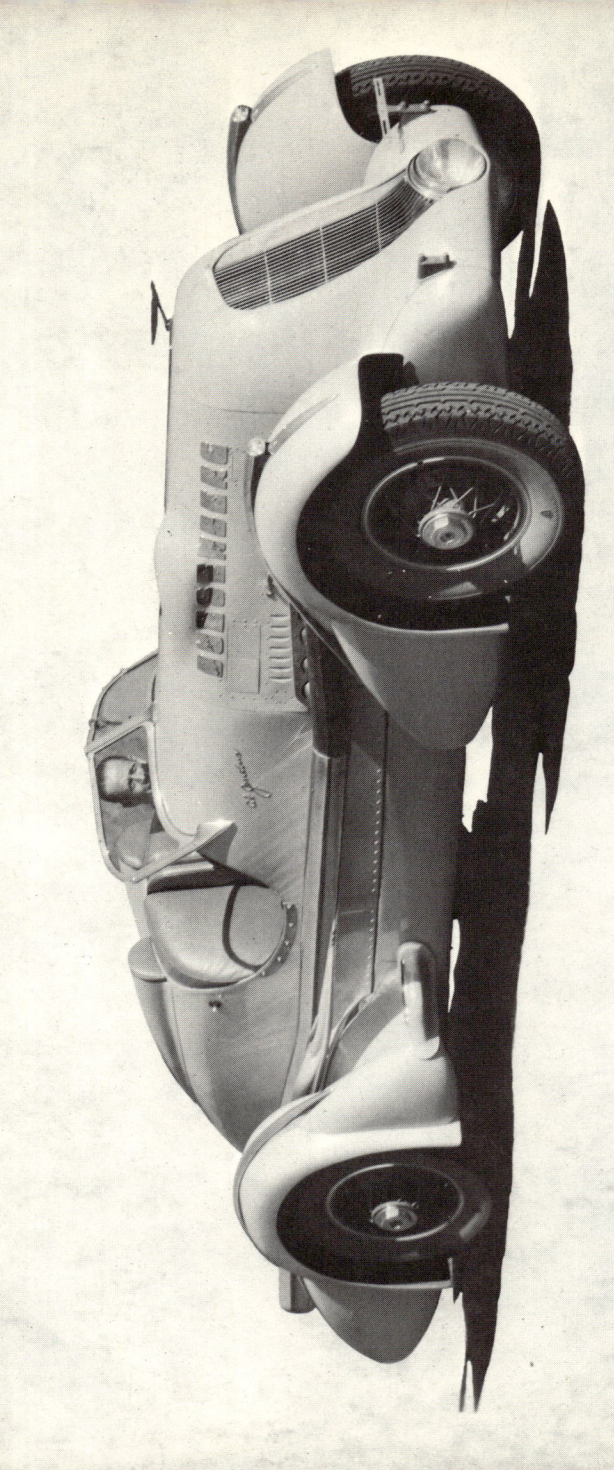

Facade of the "Mormon Meteor". Special radiator was handmade of individual lengths of tubing; a style also adapted to the special Walker-Le Grande coupe for Eli Lilly. (*Photo, J. Herbert Newport*)

gan to suffer from a slipping clutch and he dropped back, ultimately to finish sixth.

As the last laps drew near, Murphy still clung to the lead, with virtually no cooling for his engine. In the last lap he pulled into the pits for tires, but didn't dare open the radiator cap and he sped off with the instruction to "go slow". As long as he could keep moving the race was his for his determined, gallant driving had won him a full fifteen minutes over Ralph

Ab Jenkins record car had an aerodynamic design of high efficiency, but it was also a stylish automobile and attracted attention wherever it was seen. (*Photo, J. Herbert Newport*)

THE DUESENBERG

De Palma's Ballot. Much to the French disdain, he did keep moving and crossed the finish line first and to the same stony silence which the French spectators had given the German victory in the 1914 edition of the Grand Prix. Needless to say, there was a rather different reaction in the Duesenberg pits.

Duesenberg's racing stars were apparently in the right configuration in the 1920s for it was in this period that their most spectacular track successes were recorded. The elusive dream which Fred Duesenberg had dreamed for so many years finally came to pass in 1924—a first place in the Indianapolis "Five Hundred", with repeat performances in 1925 and 1927. The 1924 Indianapolis car was a smaller, 122-cubic-inch version of the Model A and was co-driven to victory by Joe Boyer and L. L. Corum.

In ironic contrast to the Model A, which was certainly exploited fully on the track, rather little was officially done with the even hotter J and SJ in competition. The one grand project undertaken was a very special car which became famous as the "Mormon Meteor". This speed record car, which was built three years after the death of Fred Duesenberg, began as an idea of the Cord Corporation to cook up some publicity. The company hired a top record driver named "Ab" Jenkins to drive the special car created by Augie Duesenberg who had succeeded his brother Fred as Chief Engineer.

Although most of his career was spent in the shadow of his illustrious brother Fred, Augie Duesenberg was a highly talented and creative engineer, as the "Mormon Meteor" project proved. Augie started off with a standard SJ chassis on the 142.5-inch-wheelbase frame and then "revised" the engine to

Duesenberg at speed. The "Mormon Meteor" record car streaks across the Bonneville Salt Flats to set a 24-hour average speed of 135.5 MPH and a one-hour average of 152.145 MPH. Inset is Ab Jenkins, the record driver. (*Photo, J. Herbert Newport*)

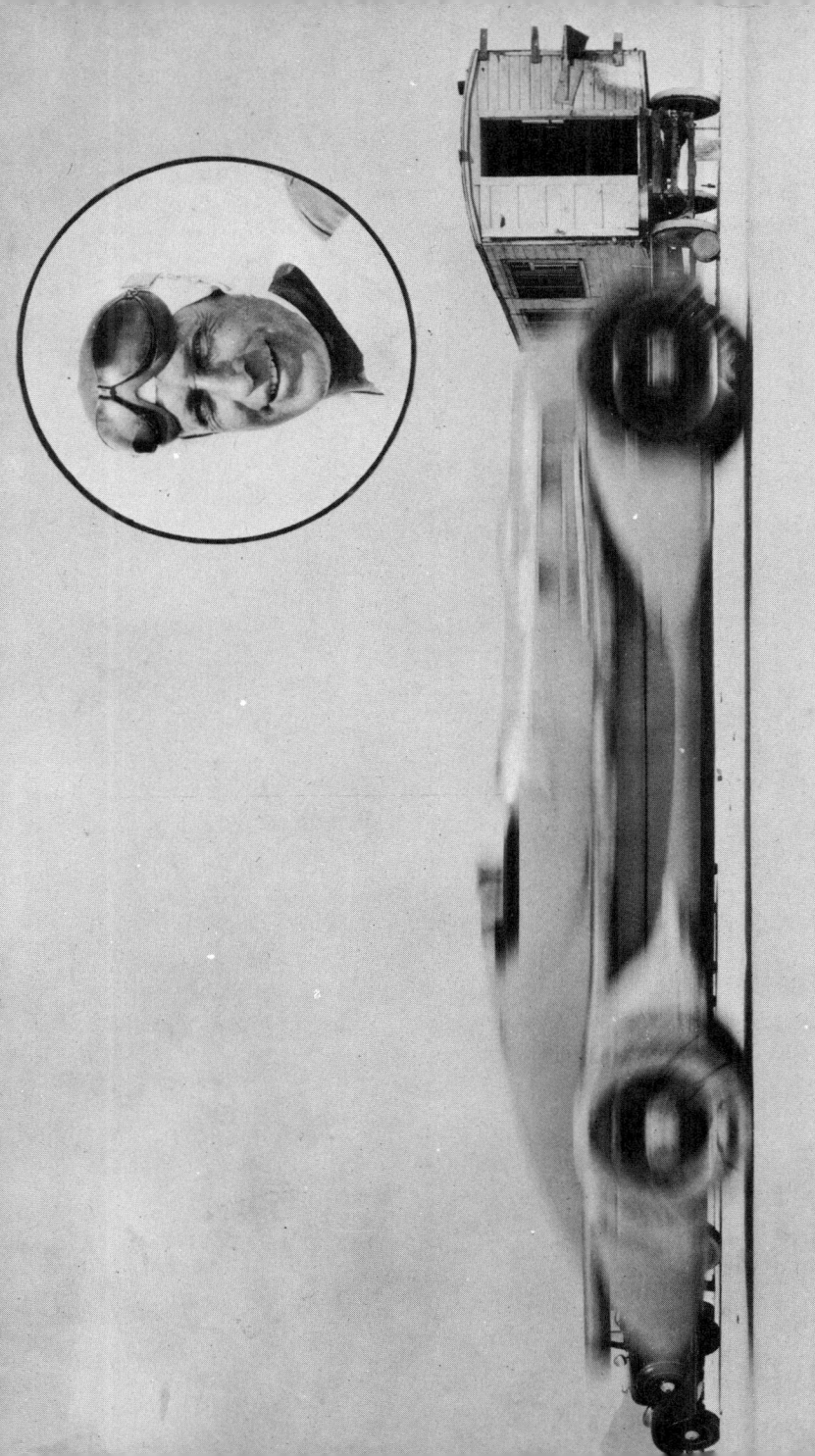

The Duesenberg

yield some 400 horsepower and 5000 RPM by means of twin carburetors, reworked manifolding, and a 3:1 final drive ratio. When he finished, a new tachometer reading to 8000 RPM and a new speedometer to 200 MPH were installed.

With the mechanical revisions complete, the Duesenberg chassis was ideally suited for a record run attempt. However, creating the highly specialized coachwork for a record setting car which also had to be suitable for ordinary street use for publicity purposes was entirely another matter. The challenge of producing such a body fell to a young body designer in the Duesenberg organization named J. Herbert Newport. One Saturday morning Newport got a call to come to Duesenberg president Harold Ames's office, and there found an optimistic fellow named David Abbot Jenkins—"Ab" for short—who wanted to drive "the world's fastest Duesenberg".

Jenkins was not overly knowledgeable about technical automotive design and construction, or particularly concerned about how the world's fastest Duesenberg would look beyond the basics. As far as he was concerned, the car merely had to be aerodynamic for speed and readily convertible for street use. So, Herb Newport was left with nearly a free hand to create the most singular Duesenberg of them all. Exactly one week later he had translated inspiration, and perspiration, into a full layout of drawings which pictured a svelte, menacing looking machine. Jenkins approved the plans *carte blanche* except for the location of the driver's step plate which was then faired into the rear fender. Newport then went to work with the metal shop foreman, a man who could do almost anything with a sheet of aluminum, and the end result was a fascinating example of specialized coachwork which certainly must rank with Andre Dubonnet's tulipwood bodied "Targa Florio" Hispano-Suiza.

The Jenkins special had an aerodynamic design of high efficiency, but it was a stylish automobile as well, and attracted a

Exotic rear view of the record; a fascinating example of specialized coachwork which must rank with Andre Dubonnet's famous tulipwood Targa Florio car. (*Photo, J. Herbert Newport*)

great deal of attention wherever it was shown to promote the name Duesenberg, Firestone tires, or other accessories. The requisite of transforming a record car into a road car was not an easy matter, but it was neatly done with special bumpers, fenders, horns, and lights which could be bolted on. Perhaps the most intriguing of these conversion accessories was a slip-in muffler which could be inserted into the *six inch* tailpipe for normal road use.

In the summer of 1935 the "Mormon Meteor" was sent to the land of its namesake and was put on a ten-mile circle in the Bonneville Salt Flats. Jenkins pushed the car around and around the ring at faster and faster speeds, finally hitting 160 MPH for awhile. After the runs were over the Duesenberg was

The Duesenberg

heavily encrusted with snow-white salt and looked as if it had been battling a blizzard instead of a desert. But it had done its duty, and took the International Class B record for twenty-four hours at an average speed of 135.5 MPH and another record of 152.145 MPH for one hour. Cameras clicked and champagne corks popped. However, the glory was short lived for later that year an Englishman came to the Utah salt flats with a record car called "Speed of the Wind" powered by a twelve-cylinder Rolls-Royce airplane engine. With this car Captain Eyston broke the Duesenberg twenty-four-hour record by a mere five miles an hour and the one-hour record by about seven miles an hour. Although it was bitterly disappointing to have the record fall in so short a time, even the defeat was a credit to Duesenberg since it took a strictly non-production chassis powered by a mammoth aero engine to beat the Duesenberg record by a scant few miles per hour. While the English car was totally conceived as a record run car, the Duesenberg was basically only a step away from a standard production car.

By 1935, Duesenberg had crested the zenith of its career, and the record run at Bonneville in a way solidified its status as the most successful fast car ever to emerge from America. Among its laurels, Duesenberg could count a pair of world's speed records, three first places in the Indianapolis "Five Hundred", and the distinction of having been the first American car ever to win a European *grande épreuve*. A few years ago in his *Kings of the Road*, Ken Purdy summed up the story of Duesenberg at speed: "No racing car ever built in America has a record comparable to the Duesenberg's. At one time or another Duesenberg cars held records ranging from the standing kilometer to that for the greatest distance covered in twenty-four hours. They competed in twenty-seven major races and placed in twenty-four of them, and ran at Indianapolis twenty times between 1912 and 1935."

7

The Legend Lives On

We began this book by calling the Duesenberg America's premier car. That is perhaps pretty strong stuff, but the Duesenberg has always seemed to live up to the grand legend which has grown around it. Legends grow easily out of such concoctions as civilized seven-litre, double overhead-camshaft engines under some of the most strikingly beautiful coachwork ever mounted on a chassis. Fred and August Duesenberg did not necessarily set out to build a legend. They simply set out to build the best car they could (with considerably more modesty than the company's advertising would indicate), and this car was to represent the highest technology of the times, the best craftsmanship, and was intended to give about ten years of superlative service. What the brothers and E. L. Cord ended up with was not only the car which they started out to create, but also a genuine institution. For American luxury car customers in the 1930s there was a considerably wider choice than the "three Cs" of the 1960s, yet for the man who wanted and could afford the *ultimate* it was simply a question of deciding on just what sort of Duesenberg he had in mind. That, gentlemen, is an institution.

Presentation of the 1966 Duesenberg. One specimen of the car was produced and the prototype was sold at auction for $37,500. (*Photo, C. McCord Purdy*)

Neither legends nor institutions die easily, and the Duesenberg aura endures as hale and hearty as some of the forty-year-old veterans which have now outlasted their alloted lifespans four times over. It is a mildly incredible phenomena that an automobile which hasn't been manufactured since 1937 can still evoke such pride and passion, a distinction shared perhaps only with Bugatti and the original Bentleys. Entrepreneurs have not been unaware of the vitality and magic of the Duesenberg name. In 1947, Marshal Merkes bought all that remained of the Duesenberg empire, principally spare parts and the Duesenberg name, and he entertained aspirations to build new Duesenbergs.

This first attempt to revive the marque called upon the talents of August Duesenberg, who envisioned a traditionally big and imposing eight-cylinder machine up-dated with the advantages of fuel injection rather than carburetion. August Duesenberg can be credited with recognizing a wave of the future when he saw it—fuel injection in automobiles was a very

82-inch hood on the revived Duesenberg harked back to the long, status producing bonnets of the 1930s. (*Photo, C. McCord Purdy*)

Classic revival radiator was focal point of the 1966 Duesenberg. (*Photo, C. McCord Purdy*)

Diligent detectives still occasionally turn up a forgotten Duesenberg tucked away in a Vermont barn or out behind a Texas bunkhouse. But even such neglected hulks as these respond to tender loving care and elbow grease.

The Legend Lives On

avant garde notion in 1947—although his fascination is intriguing in view of the fact that Fred was supposed to have been on the track of an "entirely new system of carburetion" which promised vast increases in mileage.

The speculation over engineering detail proved to be entirely academic since the world of the late 1940s promised to be so inhospitable to a new $25,000 Duesenberg that the project was shelved. Unlike the period just after World War I which merged new engineering and construction techniques, war profits, and a general joie de vivre among customers to create a Camelot for great cars, the days after World War II saw a severe retrenchment on grand cars (translation: they vanished on this side of the Atlantic) and a heavy emphasis on production of more ordinary automobiles.

The 1960s were another story altogether. Cars were being pumped out of Detroit at a rate which promised to turn the country into a coast to coast parking lot under a three thousand mile cloud of hydrocarbons. The far-out, finned styles of the late 1950s had given way to a boxy sameness among automobiles which even began to spread to the curve-conscious Europeans. With problems of basic transportation a thing of the past, larger numbers of Americans began to look at the automobile as something more than a means between Point A and Point B. Some rejected the climate controlled, spongy soft, rolling womb substitute as the ideal car for everybody and recalled that the automobile could be—as it once was—a very personal and self expressive device. Others discovered that the automobile, in its highest form, could be a legitimate work of art—a view shared even by stalwarts like Sothby's and Parke-Bernet who began to auction Duesenbergs and Bugattis *et al* along with the Rembrandts and Picassos. Prices soared dramatically, but the affluent society pretended not to notice.

In a world well supplied with cash and new found car consciousness perhaps a space age Duesenberg could finally stage

Street scene at Auburn during the A-C-D Club meeting.

A French-bodied Duesenberg attracts attention on the streets of Auburn.

An unorthodox Duesenberg rebodied in the idiom of the 1950s.

a comeback. A few people in the world of automobiles thought that it could and were willing to gamble that it would. They were Fritz Duesenberg, son and nephew of the originators; Virgil M. Exner, Sr. and his son, Detroit design consultants; Mylo Record, a Duesenberg aficionado who acted as a sort of catalyst in organizing the revival operation; and Fred McManis, Jr., who obligingly helped with some Texas cash.

Preliminary market research indicated that the automotive market could now support such a flamboyant machine as the new Duesenberg, even with its proposed $20,000 price tag. Rolls-Royce sells five hundred cars a year on the American market in that range, the $26,000 600 Mercedes-Benz had been an enormous success, and the $14,000 300 SEL 6.3-litre Mercedes was oversubscribed shortly after its announcement; so the cash was there. The news coverage of the revived Duesen-

Reminiscence at Auburn. J. Herbert Newport pauses to reflect on his work on the "Mormon Meteor" while visitors inspect this unique record car.

berg Corporation produced a gratifying response, serious as well as nostalgic, and even turned up some dealers who wanted to handle the car. Over a year before even the first prototype was ready the company had twenty five firm orders in its files, some of them with deposits of up to $5000. It seemed that the Duesenberg's prospects had indeed freshened and that a new era of "classic revival" was about to be entered.

The new car would be big in the Duesenberg tradition, although not quite as big as its ancestors. It would have a 137½-inch wheelbase as compared with 142½ and 153-inch lengths on the original cars, although the shorter wheelbase would be

The Legend Lives On

offset by the fact that there would be rather greater overhang on the modern car than with the "wheel at every corner" technique used on the originals. Duesenberg's "man in Italy", Paul Farago (who with Dale Cosper was responsible for the engineering) would co-ordinate the construction of the frame and the mounting of the Ghia custom coachbuilt bodies. Then the semi-finished car would be shipped to America for installation of the engine and most mechanical components which were to be American to ensure parts availability.

The contemporary status of the automotive industry is such that the fledgling Duesenberg Corporation could not possibly hope to create a wholly new chassis from scratch in the style that the Brothers Duesenberg had done it, but would have to settle for a selected proprietary engine. A 440-cubic-inch Chrysler powerplant with "Torqueflite" transmission was decided on, and this unit's normal 350 horsepower was raised to 375 with carburetor alterations and electronic ignition.

Although some very fine creative thinking went into the Duesenberg for the Sixties, the car did not stand head and shoulders above its contemporaries as the Duesenberg for the Thirties had. It was not the engineering showpiece that its ancestor was in its day, although this may say more *for* the advancing state-of-the-art than it does against the modern Duesenberg. One interesting and quite sensible feature was the twin sixteen-gallon porous plastic fuel tanks, one built into each rear fender. Such tanks are safety features as pioneered on racing cars, as well as being a good use of ordinarily wasted fender space, so more trunk room is preserved. The original Duesenberg emphasis on complete instrumentation was preserved, and included a separate fuel gauge for each fender tank. Suspension was not radical; using torsion bars in front and relying upon conventional multi-leaf springs in the rear. August Duesenberg's 1947 seer-like ability to predict fuel injection was overlooked entirely and carburetion was contin-

Movie stars Marion Davies and Dolores Del Rio were satisfied owners of Duesenbergs.

ued. Modern electronic transistorized ignition was adopted, as were disc brakes—without which a 6000-pound, 375-horsepower car in modern traffic would have been folly.

The promoters were satisfied that prospective Duesenberg buyers were not primarily looking for an esoteric gem of technical sophistication. They were, much more likely, looking for the awe and aura of "the mighty Duesenberg" image which had come down through the years more magnified than diminished. It was this image which Messrs. Exner *et al* had to sus-

tain, and it was very likely that the new Duesenberg would rise or fall on this factor.

Virgil Exner, Sr. had been a Duesenberg fan from his days as a teenager in Indiana, and later pursued a career in automotive design which produced a number of special show cars as well as production designs for Pontiac, Studebaker, and Chrysler. Exner and son showed initiative and enthusiasm for the contemporary Duesenberg project, and ultimately the Duesenberg Corporation retained them to design the proto-

Greta Garbo car now owned by Peter Marvel. Photo by Ronald L. Stuckey.

type car. It was Exner's philosophy that the design concept of the car should represent a merger of the contemporary and the classic; what Exner called "a new car but with enough borrowed from the old to satisfy the nostalgic".

Unfortunately, not quite enough was borrowed, for the finished design leaned quite heavily on the contemporary. The fifteen working designs for the new Duesenberg attempted to revive vestiges of clamshell fenders, rear hinged doors, an imposing eighty-two-inch hood fully a foot and a half longer than any other U.S.-made hood, and a genuine visible, vertical radiator. The last feature was probably the strong point of the various designs and may well have influenced the pseudo-classic frontal facade of the Mark III Continental. Overall, the *de novo* Duesenberg designs suggested interesting and even exotic automobiles, but somehow without the indefinable cachet of the originals.

Greta Garbo car now owned by Peter Marvel. Photo by Ronald L. Stuckey.

The Legend Lives On

On the other hand, an all-out authentic replica of the original Duesenberg also probably would not have been a sound approach, despite the success of "replicars" such as Brooks Stevens's Excalibur SS and the 1750 Zagato Alfa Romeo. Both of these are basically fun cars (if you have a large budget for fun) and were never intended to be quite the same sort of status symbol as a space age Duesenberg in which the accent would be on luxury and prestige. While it is of course much easier to judge such efforts in retrospect, it would seem that the designers overlooked the lessons of such cars as the Silver Cloud I and II Rolls-Royces, their companion Bentleys, and the Mercedes-Benz 300 S Grand Touring cabriolet and the 300 D sedan. These and a few other cars of the 1950s were notably successful at blending the contemporary and classic schools of design without offense to either.

The interior of the new Duesenberg was perhaps the high point of the project, for the intervening years permitted a level of technical sophistication, amenities, and safety never dreamed of in Fred Duesenberg's day. For instance, all the knobs, switches, and potential protruding hazards of the 1930s were replaced with padding and recessed instruments, switches, and handles. The famous full Duesenberg instrumentation was retained, even to the altimeter and stop-watch/ elapsed-time clock, all nestled in padded leather instead of the original engine-turned oxidized nickel dash panel. The commodious rear compartment was now planned for installation of television, stereo, tape recorder, telephone, and refrigerated bar. And the old touches of *le grande luxe* were not overlooked either. There was abundant use of genuine walnut wainscotting, including a flip-up writing desk. The old insistence on the best materials was preserved, so that the customer could

The Gentleman's Speedster—for Jackie Coogan.

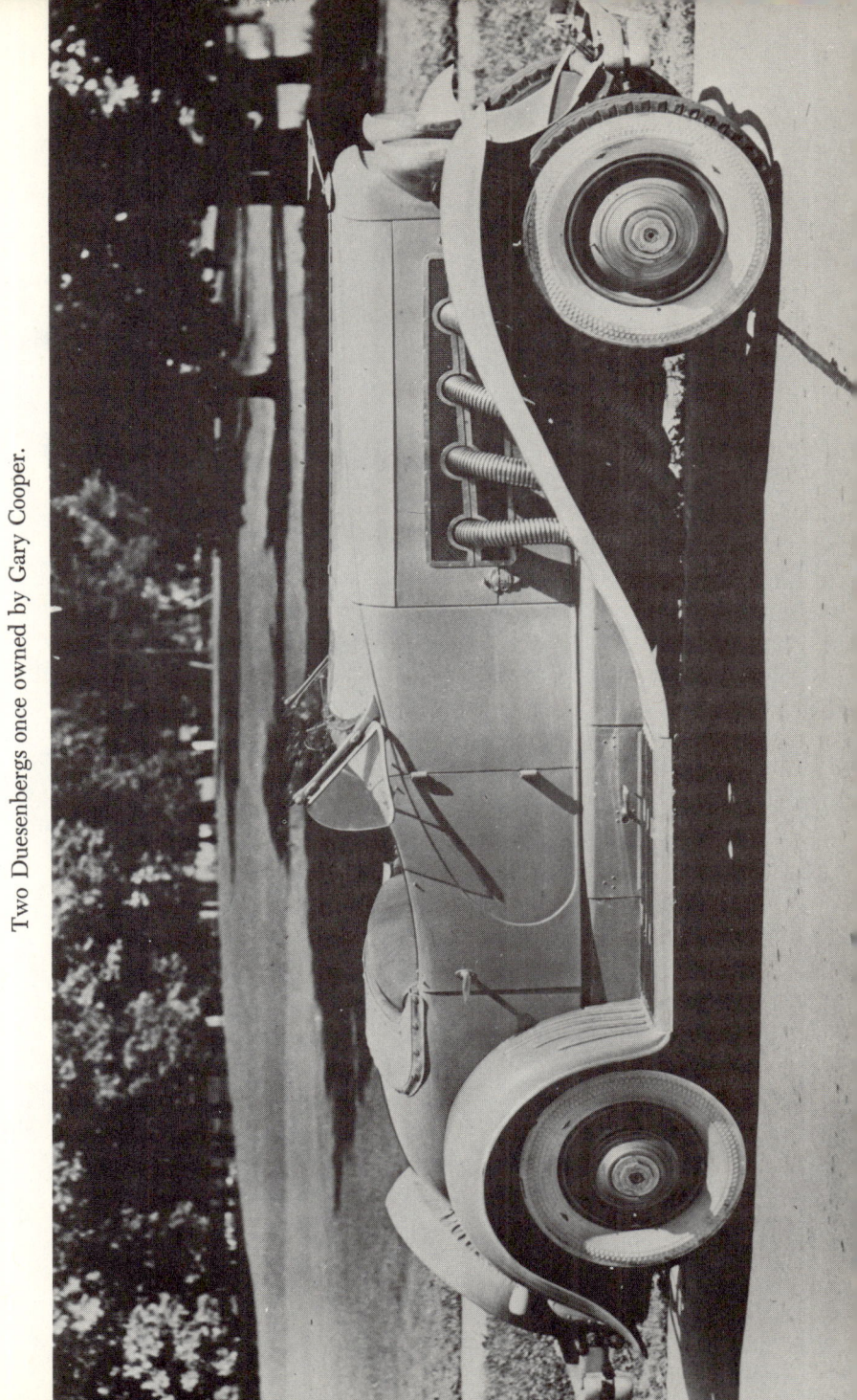

Two Duesenbergs once owned by Gary Cooper.

choose from a range of European mouton carpeting, English cashmere broadcloth, hand finished German leather from a 200-year-old tannery.

Introduction of the new Duesenberg was planned for 1966/67, but never officially happened because the company ran into that seemingly eternal bugaboo of visionary automotive endeavours, insurmountable financing problems. The Duesenberg Corporation diplomatically kept mum, but the end was obviously at hand when the company put its single completed prototype car on Parke-Bernet's auction block in Brookline, Massachusetts, on May 27th, 1968. As the sole survivor of the latest attempt to revive Duesenberg, the big maroon sedan was a choice collector's showpiece and fetched $37,500 from Mr. Harry Resnick of Ellenville, New York, a television antenna tycoon who has invested in some sixty classic cars in the space of four years. "I used to go to Las Vegas a couple of times a year;" he explained between multiple purchases at the sale, "now I do this."

As an epilogue, it seems a pity that some revival of the Duesenberg in the grand manner has not been successful so far, for it would be a unique boon to American motoring prestige. It is a continuing irony that since 1937 the world's leading producer of automobiles has had no grand marque or traditional counterpart to England's Rolls-Royce or Germany's Mercedes-Benz.

Until that day when America's only grand marque car is successfully revived, the custody for the three hundred or so heirs to the title resides with the Auburn-Cord-Duesenberg Club. The A–C–D Club—a rallying point "for those who have never relished the commonplace"—is made up of about twelve hundred people dedicated to the "restoration and preservation of Auburn, Cord, and Duesenberg automobiles". Some are associated with the automotive industry as designers, engineers, writers, mechanics, or as dealers for a variety of cars ranging

The Legend Lives On

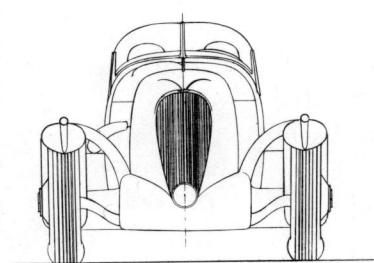
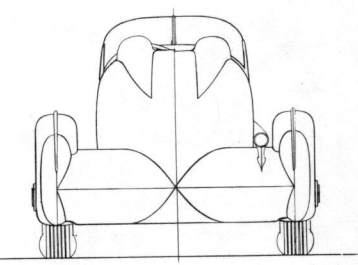

Original drawings for famous speedster driven by race driver Ab Jenkins. Designed by J. Herbert Newport in 1934.

from Ford to Rolls-Royce. Others list such diverse and nontechnical callings as clergyman, ski instructor, student, police constable, evangelist, igloo contractor, housewife, and mayor—but all are united in their fervent devotion to the cars of their marque. Once every year a large number of them convene at their "ancestral home" at Auburn, Indiana, for a parade, reunion, Concours d'Elegance, and confab. There, on that special weekend, you may find a mechanic confidently arguing a fine point of chassis detail with a millionaire collector, or a teenager enlightening his seniors with a learned dissertation on the Duesenberg system of supercharging.

Of all the various marque clubs, the Auburn-Cord-Duesenberg Club is one of the most energetic, well organized, and devoted. The members are spread across the United States and in fourteen foreign countries, and include a good percentage of the people who made original contributions to the greatness of Auburn, Cord, and Duesenberg cars. Such Honorary Members include the following: Harold T. Ames, President of Duesenberg and later Executive Vice-President of the Auburn Automobile Company; Gordon M. Buehrig, Duesenberg body designer and later Head of Styling of the Auburn Automobile Co.; Erret Lobban Cord, the man who re-developed the Auburn empire and asked the Duesenberg brothers to build "the finest thing on four wheels"; Peter De Paolo, Duesenberg racing driver who became the first winner of the Indianapolis "500" to average over 100 MPH (1925); Mrs. Gertrude Duesenberg, widow of August Duesenberg; Harry Hartz, Duesenberg racing driver; J. Herbert Newport, Duesenberg coachwork designer; Philip O. Wright, designer of the L 29 Cord.

Despite the fact that there has been no regular production of Duesenberg automobiles for over a generation, thanks to people like the members of the A–C–D Club there can really be no end to the Duesenberg story. Even today when the supply of unrestored cars has evaporated to the point that people

The Legend Lives On

are restoring 1942 Fords, diligent "detectives" still occasionally turn up a forgotten Duesenberg tucked away in a Vermont barn or out behind a Texas bunkhouse. After the restorer has worked his multi-talented magic, even the most neglected hulk can re-emerge in all its old glory. Today, chassis are even being completely re-bodied to replace damaged or less desirable coachwork with exciting roadsters or imperious dual cowl phaetons.

The percentage of J and SJ Duesenbergs surviving is relatively high, perhaps only surpassed by that of the legendary eight-litre Bentley, but the demand far exceeds this limited supply with the result that prices rise with sometimes alarming alacrity. No less an authority than Ken Purdy predicts that the time is not far off when prices for pristine classics of the first rank will be quoted in six figure sums. The money would probably not much impress Fred Duesenberg; his mind seldom ran to finance except when the lack of it interfered with building automobiles. But the fact that a whole new generation still recognizes his cars as "the finest thing on four wheels" would please him, which is perhaps the best monument that he could have.

About the Authors

Louis William Steinwedel is well-known to readers of national automotive magazines in which his articles appear regularly. When not engaged in this activity, he works at the Law in Baltimore, Maryland.

J. Herbert Newport, also a Marylander, continues to find expression for his creative talents even though his career as designer of Duesenbergs ended years ago. He rebuilds classic and antique cars for fun and profit.